rossendots

sweet fern = chiggers, but good +

3 → tip of stem = lobed, tothed less Tlan 1/3

chambered pith
- ex black walnut

A Key to the Woody Plants
of the New Jersey Pine Barrens

stipule - at base of petiole > that makes a Holly
- thornlike

ather like leaf = live thru winter.

plum / cherry = cyanide
almond smell

A Key to the Woody Plants of the New Jersey Pine Barrens

Michael D. Geller

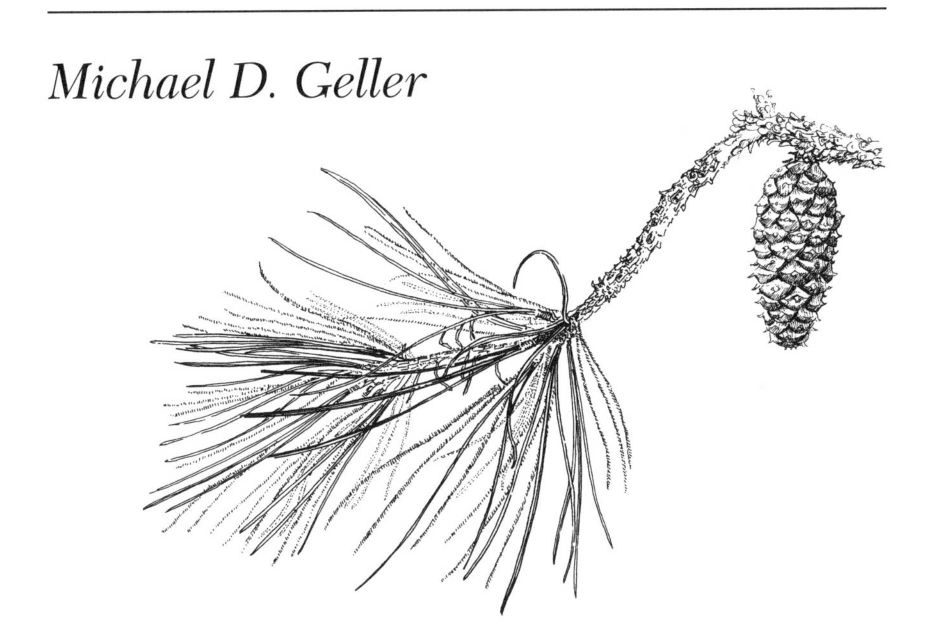

Rutgers University Press
New Brunswick, New Jersey, and London

Library of Congress Cataloging-in-Publication Data

Geller, Michael D., 1943–
A key to the woody plants of the New Jersey Pine Barrens / Michael D. Geller.
p. cm.
Includes bibliographical references (p.) and index.
ISBN 0-8135-3134-9 (cloth : alk. paper)—ISBN 0-8135-3135-7 (pbk. : alk. paper)
1. Woody plants—New Jersey—Pine Barrens—Identification. I. Title.

QK175 .G35 2002
582.16′09749′61—dc21

2002023716

British Cataloging-in-Publication data for this book is available from the British Library.

Manufactured in the United States of America

Contents

Acknowledgments

Sandy Bierbrauer's suggestion began this project several years ago. When she first commented that a key I had designed for students might be expanded into a more comprehensive work, I blanched. But her persistence, coupled with that of my wife, Ilze, began what I thought would be a relatively short project. Two years later, I approach completion.

Several people and institutions deserve mention. The late Stanley Smith, who initially pushed me toward biology, was an important influence. Along the way, many others encouraged me, none with more vigor, and none with more than his share of frustration, than John J. Christian, my mentor at SUNY—Binghamton. Gerry Moore, a former student of mine, is currently at the Brooklyn Botanic Garden. He has been inordinately patient and helpful with suggestions and answers to my questions. The same can be said for Sandy Bierbrauer. Their experience with the flora of the Pine Barrens towers over my own, and I appreciate their willingness to help with problems I have encountered while writing this. Of course, the responsibility for any errors or omissions in this work is my own.

Richard Stockton College of New Jersey supported my efforts with a Distinguished Faculty Fellowship. Dr. Vera King Farris, president of the college, also supported the publication of this work. She came through when I needed her support the most, and I appreciate her generosity.

While many have helped make this work possible, two people have made it worthwhile—my wife, Ilze, and my daughter, Lija. Their support, understanding, and sanity were, and are, a continual source of strength for me.

A Key to the Woody Plants of the New Jersey Pine Barrens

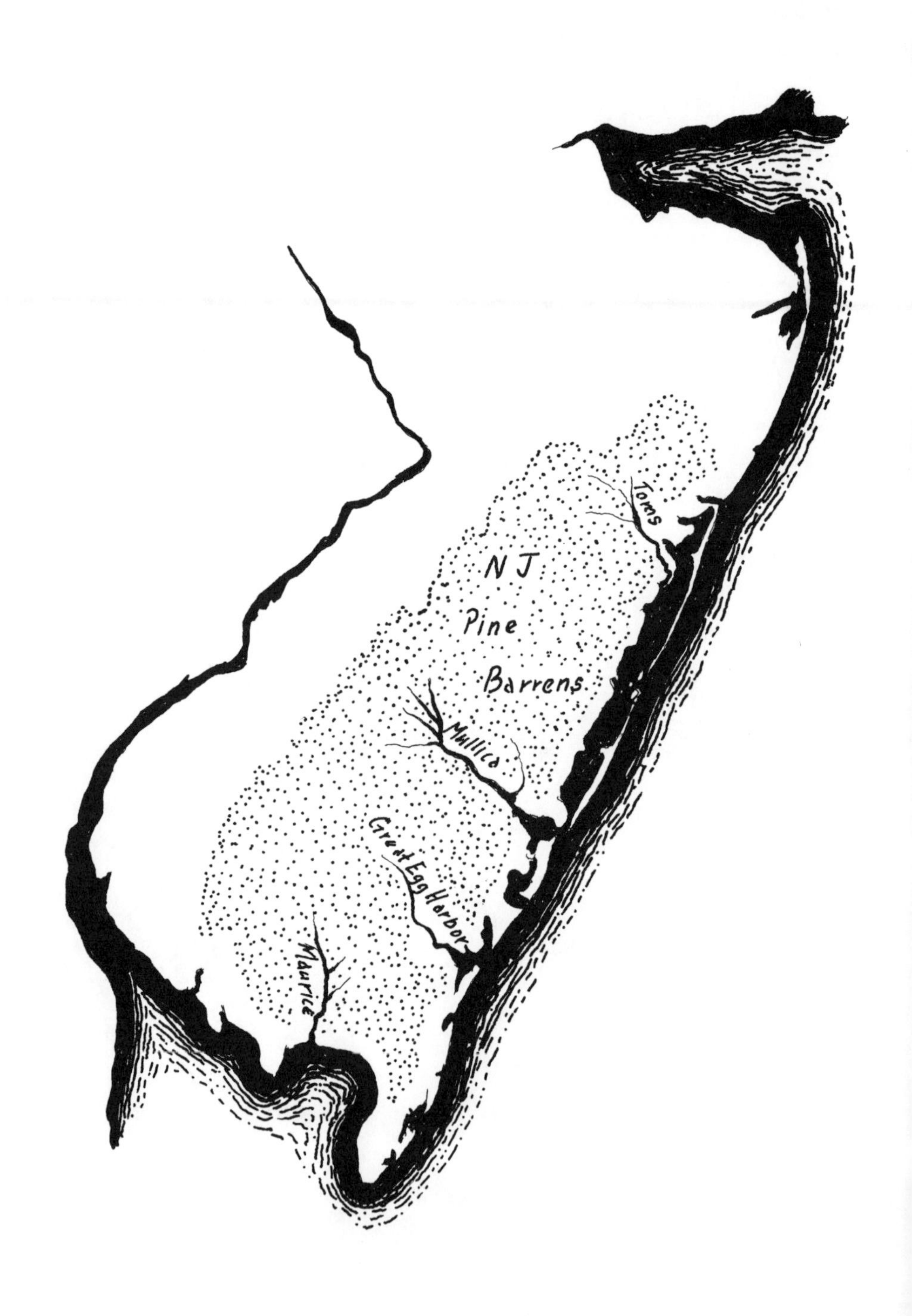
Toms
N J
Pine
Barrens
Mullica
Great Egg Harbor
Maurice

Introduction

This is a book about the woody plants of the New Jersey Pine Barrens, our country's first National Reserve. I wrote it to enable you to identify the woody plants of this area even if you have no previous experience in plant identification. While I have included some ecological information, this book is primarily a field guide that is written as a key. When I first wrote a draft several years ago, I wanted to create a key that my students could use to identify local plants while they also gained experience with keying out organisms. At the urging of several of my colleagues, I decided to expand the early draft into a book, include my own illustrations, and modify it for a broader audience.

There are many other plant guides that you might use in the Pine Barrens. However, most of these keys are designed to permit the user to identify all the woody plants of a larger region, like the eastern or northeastern United States. The New Jersey Pine Barrens are distinct in that they are "depauperate"—they lack the diversity of species found in nearby areas. Comparing your specimens to those of a larger region increases the risk of misidentification.

There are field guides to the Pine Barrens, but these are very broad in scope, providing information on many different kinds of plants and animals. Because they are so broad, they are often limited to only the more common woody plants. More importantly, field guides rely heavily on pictures and descriptions. With a key, you proceed in a logical fashion, using a step-by-step process to the correct identification.

This book lists all of the woody plants of the Pine Barrens except for a very few rare species that were recently introduced from outside the area. You do not need to have a background in botany or science to use this key. Many of you may never have had a college botany course. Others may have gone through that experience only to discover, years later, you have forgotten most of what you once learned. In writing this book, I have tried to make it as accessible as possible by using plain English. Like most technical fields, botany has a complex vocabulary to describe various features of plants. By replacing these terms with phrases that anyone can understand, this key becomes far more user-friendly for the lay person.

I have tried to make the job of identifying plants simpler in another respect. Most keys and field guides include descriptions of the plants, but these are located outside the body of the key. To confirm your identification, you must flip to another page and read a lengthy description of the species. In this book, these accounts are placed within the body of the key. It makes the key longer, but you can immediately compare the description to your specimen and rapidly confirm your identification. I have also included pen and ink drawings of many of the common species to further help you identify our local plants. These should give you greater confidence in your identifications.

I limited this key to the woody plants for several reasons. These plants are common and easy to find. The number of species is limited compared to that for herbaceous plants—those with fleshy stems. Because of their diversity and obscure traits, herbaceous plants can be much more difficult to identify. Often, you must obtain a specimen while it is in flower, which occurs only for a short time during the growing season.

The situation regarding woody plants is much different. Because there are fewer species, we can identify these plants using a wide variety of features, including leaf shape, branching pattern, features of the buds, and other anatomical traits. Also, woody plants retain many important features over winter. All this makes woody plants much easier to identify. While the thought of making sense of what grows in the pine woods might seem awesome at first, within a short period of time you will recognize common species. In time, you may know them all.

Learning how to key out woody plants is a useful beginning for an amateur botanist and a pleasant hobby that brings you outdoors. Taking a sample from a woody plant usually does not harm the plant and may actually stimulate growth. Finally, knowing the woody plants of the Pine Barrens enhances your understanding of the ecology of this unique area. It can also provide some practical information since environmentally important areas like wetlands are often easily identified using woody plants. Once you can recognize the woody plants that grow in wetland areas, these places will be much easier to identify.

You will need very little to begin identifying the plants. I recommend that you bring a small penknife to cut samples and occasionally slice into a plant to expose some of its features. You will also need a small magnifying glass or hand lens. Most stationery or office supply stores sell these. If you are more serious, buy a good hand lens, or loupe (either a Hastings or a Coddington triplet or doublet). These can be purchased from several supply companies (Ben Meadows Company; Forestry Supplies, Inc.; or New Jersey's own Edmund Scientific in Barrington). As of this writing, hand lenses run from under $10 to over $40. Although it might seem like a good idea, do not buy one that magnifies too much, that is, anything over 10x (or a tenfold magnification). A hand lens that magnifies too much or has too small a diameter (distance across the face of the lens) and collects less light is hard to use under field conditions. The important point is clarity and ease of use, not total magnification. I use a 7x Hastings triplet (i.e., made up of three lenses), which cost about $36 when I bought it several years ago.

In writing this book, I have tried to provide all the information a beginner might need to start identifying woody plants. In simplifying much of the terminology, I did not intend to slight my readers. Rather, I have tried to make the experience of learning how to identify these plants as painless as possible. Those of you who are familiar with the natural history and geology of the Pine Barrens of New Jersey may find chapter 1 unnecessary. Those who are more experienced with the important features of woody plants can skim chapter 2, and you may omit chapter 3 if you are an experienced user of dichotomous keys.

Before we begin, three caveats. First, you will need to know which plants not to touch. In our area, poison ivy (*Toxicodendron radicans,* Fig. 1) and poison sumac (*T. vernix*) should be avoided for obvious reasons. Poison ivy can be ivylike, or vinelike, in form, but it can also grow as a shrub. There is some poison oak (*T. toxicarium*) in the southern portion of the Pine Barrens. This looks much like poison ivy except that it only grows as a shrub and typically has more lobed and rounded leaves. Not only should you not touch the plants; you should avoid touching anything that comes in contact with them. Most other plants can be safely handled.

Second, take a large sample size when you begin keying out a plant. Start by taking several branches, each one to two feet long. When you begin trying to decide whether or not a plant has a certain feature, you are going to need to look at *several* leaves, leaf scars, or buds. Examining only one leaf or one bud may lead you to the wrong conclusion. The more of the plant you can examine, the more confident you will be in your identification. Because you may have to remove leaves, buds, or a portion of the stem to find some features, you may well be "whittling down" your sample as you work. I cannot overstress the need to have a nice large sample and to thoroughly examine it. A short twig with one or two leaves is not going to exhibit enough easily identifiable features, especially since not every leaf or bud may be representative. Of course, the best approach is to use this key in the field with the plant right in front of you rather than remove a sample for future examination. That way, you can look at the whole plant and find features that may not be apparent in a small sample. Also, your sample will be fresh and in good condition.

Third, many ornamental and agricultural plants are not covered in this key. I have made exceptions for those species that have become established in the wild as escapees. However, a few ornamental species may have been planted around buildings that are no longer standing. These plants may even propagate locally. But if they have not spread and are not widely distributed in the New Jersey Pine Barrens, I have not included them in this key.

Identifying the woody plants of this region is not as daunting a task as it might first seem. The New Jersey Pine Barrens are not ecologically diverse, so there are relatively fewer species than in many other regions. While you might have to key out a certain plant several times, you will begin to recognize it by sight within a short while. Understanding which plants might have medicinal properties or edible berries, which are found in wet or disturbed areas, or which are used by animals for food increases your appreciation of the ecology of this unusual area, New Jersey's Pine Barrens.

Chapter 1

Why the Pine Barrens Are Barren

As you enter the New Jersey Pine Barrens from almost any direction, you are struck by how different the vegetation is compared to the forest of most surrounding areas. Even if your experience in plant ecology is limited to an occasional walk in a park, the differences between what you see elsewhere in the northeastern United States and what you encounter in the Pine Barrens cannot be missed. Here, the trees are shorter, and the pines more gnarly and shaggy. The forest looks more monotonous, and in some respects, it is. Compared to the woody plants in the vicinity of New York (Gleason 1962), there are about 30 percent fewer species in the Pine Barrens. In addition, there are fewer types of ecological communities, and in most of these the variety of species is less than what you might find in more typical areas.

Ecologists call this variety "species diversity," and compared to most forests in the Northeast, the New Jersey Pine Barrens certainly have low species diversity. The lack of diversity is related to another quality of these forests, one that lends its very name to the area. But this name begs a question. Why is it that this area of southern New Jersey is covered by pine forests with low species diversity? In other words, why is it that the Pine Barrens are barren?

This is a simple question with a simple answer, at least on first inspection. This area is the way it is because the soils are poor. They contain a very high proportion of sand, which affects both the chemical and the physical nature of the soils, making them drought-prone, nutrient-deficient, and acidic. To understand why our sandy soils have these properties, we must examine their characteristics more closely.

One important physical feature of soils is their ability to hold water. This is related to the size of the particles in the soil. The largest of these are stones and pebbles, collectively called "gravel" by soil scientists. Particles of gravel are larger than two millimeters (about the diameter of a conventional lead pencil). Sand particles are smaller than gravels but larger than 0.05 mm. Because you can actually feel individual sand particles, soils containing sands feel gritty. Coarse sands are very rough, but even in fine sands with a particle size just over 0.05 mm, you can still detect the individual sand grains. The other two soil particles are silts and clays. When you rub silts and clays between your fingers, they feel smooth, a bit like talcum powder. You cannot feel individual silt or clay particles with your fingers because they are smaller than the distance between the nerve endings. Your mouth, however, is more sensitive. You may have felt grit when you have eaten a vegetable that you thought you had cleaned thoroughly only to discover that your mouth can detect what your fingers have missed. The vegetable you thought was clean actually contained particles of silt.

You are not likely to find dry clay in the Pine Barrens because in our area it does not stay dry enough long enough to remove the water that tightly adheres to the very small particles that make up clayey soils. When wet, clays and silts can be molded into shapes. Of course, clay is very malleable, and it will hold complex shapes. Soils dominated by silts are not as moldable, they hold their shapes less well, and they break apart under pressure.

The size of the soil particles affects how well the soil holds water. Sands have large-sized particles with correspondingly large spaces between them. These large spaces act as channels, permitting water to move rapidly through the soil. On the other hand, soils with larger amounts of silts drain less well and hold moisture better than sands because their smaller particle size creates many small channels, which retard the flow of water. Clays, the smallest soil particles, often hold water too well. Their very small size creates many tiny channels for water to move through. In addition, clay particles are much smaller than those of sand or silt, and for a given volume of soil, there are many more clay particles. The total surface area of these particles far exceeds the total surface area of the same volume of sand or silt. Water binds to the surfaces of soil particles, and it binds very tightly to the greater surface area of a given volume of clay. As a result, clays can almost completely impede the flow of water. The best soils contain an even mix of all three particle sizes. Thus, they retain water well enough to permit plants to extract it but do not hold water so well as to become water-logged. These soils are called "loams."

Most of the soils of the Pine Barrens are classified as sands, loamy sands, and sometimes sandy loams, depending on their percentages of sands, silts, and clays. Soils that are mostly silts and clays are relatively rare in the Pine Barrens, although scattered deposits exist in certain areas. Clay deposits, called "clay lenses," are of much ecological and practical significance because they retard the movement of water through them, leading to the formation of wetlands. Often, this happens in places where you really do not expect to find wetlands, like the higher elevations away from streams and ponds. Clay lenses also separate underground aquifers into separate, water-containing beds.

Even though our region receives on average about 40 inches of rain a year, spread more or less equally over the seasons, most Pine Barrens soils dry out quickly because of the high proportion of sands. The coarser the sand and the higher the percentage of the sands, the more rapidly water drains through it and the less tightly water is held. As a result, sandy soils are more susceptible to drought, which is a frequent feature of a Pine Barrens summer.

Sandy soils affect plants another way; they limit the availability of nutrients. Nutrients are the chemical elements required by plants, and they include compounds like nitrates and phosphates as well as metals like magnesium. In all soils, nutrients accumulate from two sources. Debris, in the form of leaves, branches, and other plant parts, rains down from the tree and shrub canopy to the upper level of the soil year after year. Invertebrates such as insects and snails consume this material, digest what they can, and excrete the rest. Earthworms and other organisms consume what is not completely digested, but even they cannot break down all the organic material. Bacteria and fungi digest much of the organic material that might be left over. In the process of decomposing organic material, any nutrient molecules that might be present in the leaves are eventually released into the soil, where they go into solution. Plants absorb these nutrients and use them over again by taking the energy obtained from photosynthesis to make more plant biomass. However, some leftover organic material is resistant to digestion and persists in soils. This material, called "humus," builds up, especially in wetland soils, where oxygen is limiting.

Another source of nutrients is the weathering of minerals in the soil. The geological substrate from which the soil develops contains minerals, which, in turn, contain chemical elements. As this substrate is broken down by water and other agents, any chemical elements present in this parent material go into solution, where they become available to plants. Sometimes the element and the amount released are beneficial to the plant, and the mineral releases nutrients. But other minerals release chemical elements that are toxic for one of two reasons; either the amount released inhibits the growth of certain plants, or the nature of the element itself is damaging.

The sandy nature of Pine Barrens soils delivers a "double whammy" to plants. First, the nutrients that might accumulate from the breakdown of plant debris are washed away by the rapid percolation of water through the granular soil of this region. In this case, the nutrients are transported away from the roots and are therefore unavailable to plants. Second, the sands of the Pine Barrens are made up mostly of quartz, and quartz does not break down easily. When it does, it releases molecules that are not used by most plants. Feldspars, another group of minerals and one that contributes to soils surrounding the Pine Barrens, contain much higher levels of nutrients. In addition, feldspars break down easily, thus releasing nutrients that are then available to plants. In the soils of the Pine Barrens, less than one percent of the material is feldspars (Douglas and Trela 1979). As a result, there is far less input of nutrients from the natural weathering of the soils.

Sandy soils impose yet another burden on plants. These soils are notoriously acidic. In some cases, these soils are two thousand times more acidic than other soils in New Jersey (Tedrow 1979). This unusually high level of acidity is brought about by several different mechanisms.

Acidic compounds are those that easily give off the positively charged hydrogen ion (H^+). These compounds are released when organic matter is decomposed by invertebrates, fungi, and bacteria. In many soils outside of the Pine Barrens, this ion adheres to the surfaces of clay and humus particles because they contain numerous negatively charged sites. These negatively charged sites hold the positively charged hydrogen ions as well as similarly charged ions like aluminum. When enough hydrogen ions are removed, the acidity of the soil decreases. Humus and many clays actually tie up positively charged ions in such a way as to retard any change in acidity even if acid is added directly to the soil. A discussion of this process, called the "cation exchange capacity," is beyond the scope of this book except to say that our soils have a low cation exchange capacity because they typically lack the levels of humus or clay found in other, less sandy soils. Lacking negatively charged sites, our soils cannot remove, or tie up, naturally released compounds that make the soil more acidic.

The sandy nature of our soils contributes to their acidity in another way. They tend toward acidity for the same reason that they have low nutrient concentrations. Many of the organic molecules that are rapidly washed out of our soils are also negatively charged. If present, these molecules would tie up the positively charged hydrogen ions, thus reducing the acidity of the soils. But in our soils, the rapid movement of water through them washes out these organic molecules. If our soils had less sand and more clay or silt, these organic molecules would persist for longer periods of time, long enough to pick up hydrogen ions.

In addition, soils with a lot of aluminum also tend to be acid. Aluminum increases acidity by pulling apart water molecules (H_2O), binding the OH^- group, and leaving behind the positively charged hydrogen ion (H^+). Moreover, aluminum is toxic at high levels. So soils that drain quickly, that lack clays or significant amounts of humus, and that contain aluminum tend to be more acidic and inhospitable to many species of plants. Pine Barrens soils have all these features (Douglas and Trela 1979).

These droughty soils with high acidity and low levels of nutrients such as nitrogen, phosphorous, and magnesium (Tedrow 1979) contribute to the poor growing conditions. The plants that do grow in our forests often grow slowly, and they provide poor-quality browse with limited nutrients and a low protein content. One obvious result of this is the small size of adult deer in the Pine Barrens. Another result is that few plant species are adapted to these conditions, which is why these plants—mostly pines, oaks, and heathlike shrubs—dominate the forests of our region (Whittaker 1979).

A lack of topographic relief also contributes to the low species diversity of the Pinelands. Compared to much of the eastern United States, the Pine Barrens are flat. All other things being equal, areas with more varied landforms have greater diversity because they have more varied environmental conditions. South-facing slopes are warmer than north-facing slopes. Depressions might contain pockets of cooler air, collect water, and have higher humidity. The tops of hills are exposed to more air flow and are often drier, with more extremes of temperature. Erosion and other downward movement, particularly down steep hillsides, brings different materials to lower elevations and might contribute to differences in soil chemistry. A varied topography creates more varied ecological conditions through these and other mechanisms. Because the topography of the Pine Barrens is so much less pronounced than that of most of the Northeast, there is less variety in the ecological conditions and therefore, fewer species.

So the Pine Barrens contain their peculiar mix of plants because the ground is mostly flat with gentle and gradual changes in elevation and because the sandy soils contribute to aridity and acidity, and to low nutrient concentrations. But why should this area have this particular mix of characteristics, a mix that is not typical of the Northeast? If we hold that the

Pine Barrens are barren because of the topography and the sandy soils, we open the door to yet another question. Why is this area different from the rest of New Jersey and the northeastern United States? Why is our land so flat, and why are our soils so sandy? To answer this question, we must consider how the southern portion of New Jersey was formed over the course of millions of years.

There are two factors that form the surface features, or landforms, of an area. The first results in more pronounced topography by pushing the land up, through either the action of volcanoes or the buckling and upthrusting of land. The latter occurs when tectonic plates move apart or against each other over the course of hundreds of millions of years. This movement causes underground pressure that lifts portions of the land surface in a fashion similar to wrinkling a smooth blanket on a bed. As the bed is mussed up by the force applied from below or from the sides, the blanket is no longer smooth but undulating.

The second factor eventually leads to flatter landforms. Erosion wears down the land that has been pushed up. Where the action of water, wind, or ice is rapid, erosion forms more or less steep-sided gullies as material is worn away. But the material that is removed in this process has to be deposited somewhere, and at that location it forms more or less flat features with low relief. Depending on whether there is more or less material deposited, there might be slight elevations or depressions. Subsequent erosion or the rise and fall of the earth's crust might also alter the landform of these deposited materials.

What types of materials are deposited depends on two things, the nature of the source material and the force applied by whatever is causing the erosion. Ice moves slowly but exerts great force. It can move rocks the size of boulders. The movement of glaciers transports large amounts of material, leading to the deposition of "moraines"—piles left along the sides or in front of a glacier. New York's Long Island is an example of a terminal moraine formed when the Wisconsin ice sheet retreated about ten thousand years ago. Water can carry large rocks if the water is moving very rapidly and there is a lot of it. More commonly, water carries smaller particles, including sands, silts, and clays. The more rapidly the water moves, the larger the size of the soil particle it transports. Moving air exerts less force and typically carries sand, silt, and clay particles.

The surface features and soils of southern New Jersey were formed mostly by the deposition of material carried by water. One way that water helped form these soils and landforms was through the rise and fall of sea levels. Climatic cooling caused ice sheets to expand, forming huge glaciers. The volume of the oceans decreased as water was converted into ice. As climates warmed again, glaciers melted, increasing the oceans' volume to earlier levels or beyond. This change in the mass of the oceans raised and lowered sea levels such that at the height of the last glaciation, sea levels were about 300 feet lower than they are currently. In addition, our portion of the North American continent rose and fell with the movement of the earth's crust over the course of tens of millions of years. Both the advance and retreat of glaciers and the movement of the earth's crust caused the sea to advance over and retreat from southern New Jersey several times (Owens and Sohl 1969; Rhodehamel 1979). Most other areas of the Northeast were spared this fate because of their higher elevations.

As the ocean invaded and retreated from the area, it deposited coarse beach and finer bay sands, although some silts and clays were deposited in marshes. The shifting currents also formed bars and barrier islands. Some of the roads of the Pine Barrens transect these beach fronts, and you can almost imagine traveling up from the bottom of a bay to the top of a barrier island as you cross the gently rolling landscape of southern New Jersey. During this period of time, rivers cut through the area, slowly shifting their banks and beds, eroding material from one location and depositing it elsewhere as new banks and deltas.

The second way that water influenced the topography of our area was the more recent events of the last ice age. Over the past million years, large glaciers migrated from the poles into what are now temperate latitudes. The last, and most significant, glacial advance and retreat ended about ten thousand years ago. At its height, this mass of ice extended over most of Canada and the northern United States, ending as a cliff of ice approximately one mile high covering what is now New York City. The climate of southern New Jersey was much colder, and the vegetation was arctic tundra. The Pine Barrens were home to many animals that are now extinct, including giant ground sloths, dire wolves, short-faced bears, saber-toothed lions, several species of horses, mammoths, and at one time a giant beaver the size of a modern black bear. As the climate warmed, this glacier retreated as it melted, forming huge rivers, which washed down sediments, mostly coarse sands and gravels, that now cap portions of the Pine Barrens. These rivers also contributed to the landforms of southern New Jersey as they meandered back and forth over the landscape.

Our relatively flat terrain and sterile, sandy soil are the results of the action of water. Events transpiring millions of years ago influence the ecology of our area today by limiting our vegetation to species that tolerate the conditions of the Pine Barrens, conditions determined in part by the advance and retreat of ancient seas and glaciers. One of these species, arguably the dominant plant of the Pine Barrens and one that lends its very name to the place, is the pitch pine (*Pinus rigida*). This species has an influence that extends beyond its shear abundance because the pitch pine is fire-adapted. It helps make the Pine Barrens a veritable tinderbox. Few other places in the United States are as naturally combustible.

On first thought, it seems strange that a plant should increase the likelihood of fire because fire can kill plants. However, many ecosystems in the United States are maintained by periodic fires. Like all things, ecosystems are constantly changing. This change, termed "ecological succession," occurs because organisms gradually modify their surroundings. In southern New Jersey, an open area is first invaded by grasses and other nonwoody plants, which gradually build up the soil by adding organic matter and some nutrients. Grassy fields are eventually colonized by woody plants. Pitch pine seeds are carried in by the wind while those of the red cedar (*Juniperus virginiana*) are brought in by animals. Over time, these plants become more and more common, growing so close together as to crowd out competitors by limiting how much light penetrates to the soil. As a result, grasses and herbaceous species disappear because the light they need early in their life cycles diminishes. Eventually, the pitch pine comes to dominate the area by crowding out red cedar.

Alas, the pitch pine literally sows the seeds of its own demise because at some point the canopy becomes too dense, and light penetration decreases even more. When light levels fall low enough, mature pines produce seeds that cannot grow in the understory. As so often happens in ecological succession, the plant that dominates one stage has created an environment no longer hospitable to its own continuance. In southern New Jersey, gray squirrels bring in acorns from surrounding areas as they cache food for the winter. Those they forget to dig up eventually sprout. Acorns are much larger than pine seeds; the latter must be carried by the wind. In part because of their greater mass of food reserves in the seed and their larger, more efficient leaves, oaks can survive with less light than is required by pines. What started out as an open field that was taken over by pines eventually becomes a forest dominated by oaks.

But pitch pines have a countermeasure to oaks, one that helps them succeed despite the advantage oaks have. This countermeasure is fire. A few species have some features that help them survive a fire. Pitch pines have these and more. Not only do they survive fires better than oaks; they often reproduce after a fire. In addition, they actually increase the likelihood that a fire will occur.

First, the thick bark of older pitch pines shields the sensitive tissue just beneath it, making them far more fire-resistant than the thinner-barked oaks. Second, the growth of new needles is rapid, and it can happen almost anyplace on the tree. Unlike most plants, the growth of needles and twigs is not limited to the tips of branches or where there are lateral buds. In pitch pines, new tissue can develop from the trunk or sometimes from a burned or cut-down stump. You might notice the shaggy appearance of some of these trees. They do not look at all like the white pine, or most ornamental cone-bearing plants. This appearance reflects the growth of needles, twigs, and small branches along the trunk, which sometimes can be so dense as to give the tree a wooly appearance. Growth of new needles following a fire helps the pines rapidly recover the ability to photosynthesize, and this gives them an important advantage over other plants. Some of our oaks and heathlike shrubs can also recover quickly from fires, but not as well as pitch pines. Finally, some of our pines have their ecology so tied to fire that they actually require a fire to reproduce successfully.

Among pitch pines, there are two types of trees. In the first, the cones open spontaneously. In the second, the cones have to be heated to about 150 degrees Fahrenheit before opening and shedding their seeds. Pitch pines with the latter feature are said to have "serotinous" cones. Whether a pitch pine tree opens its cones spontaneously or not is controlled ultimately by its genes, and these genes help determine under what conditions the plant will reproduce most successfully.

Temperatures in the canopy as hot as 150 degrees are only achieved during a severe fire. After that happens, the cones that would normally stay closed open up and shed their seeds. These fall into an area from which fire has removed other plants, increasing both light penetration and nutrient levels. Among the plants that have been killed by the fire are young pine trees, because these are much more vulnerable to fire than older plants with thicker bark (Little 1979). In areas that are particularly fire-prone, the most successful pines are those whose cones only open after being heated. In these areas, the seedlings and saplings of pines whose cones open spontaneously are generally removed by fire. The situation is different in areas where fires are less common or less severe. In these areas, pines with serotinous cones cannot compete with those whose cones open spontaneously because without fire, serotinous cones rarely open to shed their seeds. In the complete absence of fire, oaks and other hardwoods eventually replace pines because the latter require more light.

Pines actually increase the likelihood of fires by producing abundant litter consisting of needles and branches that contain flammable resins. Other plants that grow in the Pine Barrens contribute to this process by producing litter that is high in oils and waxes. This material decomposes slowly, gradually building up in this drought-prone ecosystem. At some point, a fire begins. The fire could be started by spontaneous combustion, when decomposition creates heat; by lightning strikes; or by humans, who may set a fire deliberately or out of carelessness. Apparently, people have been starting fires in the Pine Barrens for quite some time, and there is evidence that Native Americans used fire to enhance hunting prior to the advent of Europeans (Little 1979). Whatever the cause, the naturally dry conditions of the Pine Barrens and their proximity to coastal winds cause the fires to spread. If there is significant build-up of litter, fires can be severe and extensive.

As you travel through the Pine Barrens, you move through areas that are fire-prone or fire-resistant, depending on several factors, the most significant of which is the presence of fire breaks. These include human disruption, like towns and highways, and natural fire breaks in the form of rivers and large areas of wetlands (Windisch 1999). North of Tuckerton along Ocean County Highway 539 are several areas of the Pine Barrens that are so fire-prone that only the most fire-resistant species persist. These are so affected by periodic fire that the pitch pines and a few resistant species of oak are stunted. Many are less than four feet tall even though they may be relatively old. These areas of stunted pine forest are called the Pygmy Pine Plains. One of the most spectacular is below the village of Warren Grove.

I have suggested that the Pine Barrens are largely uniform, with drought-prone soils and little variation in the kinds of plant communities. This is, of course, a gross oversimplification. Despite the generally flat topography and the relatively consistent soils, there is a good deal of variation within the Pinelands. Some of it is due to sporadic events like fires or human activities, like farming or development. Still more is due to natural change, ecological succession. Even if we exclude these agents, the Pine Barrens are far from a homogeneous continuum of pine forests. Several other types of plant communities reside here. The major factor that contributes to this variation is how wet the soils are.

In many parts of the United States, water runs off the land surface to accumulate in streams that eventually coalesce into larger bodies of water. How much runoff occurs depends on many factors, including the rate and amount of rainfall, the surface topography, and the porosity of the soils. However, surface runoff directly contributes relatively little to the rivers of the Pine Barrens because the sandy soils are so porous and also because the topography is relatively flat. Water percolates into the ground, eventually reaching the ground-water table. Below this point, the soil is saturated.

If you walk from a higher elevation to a lower one in the Pine Barrens, you are likely walking from an area where the water table may be quite deep beneath your feet toward an area where it may be much closer to the surface. The lower the elevation, the closer the water table is to the surface. Eventually, you may even reach a wetland area, where the water table is at or near the surface. Here, the ground can be completely saturated, particularly in very wet years and in the early spring, when snow melt or winter rains combine with the relative inactivity of the plants over winter to create a seasonally high water table near the soil surface.

As you continue walking downslope from wetlands, you might walk into a stream or a pond. Here, you are in an area where the ground-water table is actually above the land's surface. In many other areas of the United States, streams and ponds mark areas where surface water collects in depressions. In the Pine Barrens, we have ponds and streams in locations where the surface of the land dips below the level of the underground water table.

Above the ground-water table, the soils are generally well aerated, but below the ground-water table, the spaces between the soil particles are saturated with water. These soils are anaerobic, that is, they have very little available oxygen. Oxygen from the atmosphere is present in most surface water, because rainfall collects air, and therefore oxygen, as it falls. In a stream, water also picks up air through wave action and as it bubbles over objects. It is this oxygen that fish and other aquatic life absorb through their gills. In soils, this atmospheric oxygen is lost for two reasons: first, bacteria and other organisms use it in respiration and second, it cannot be easily replenished. Water moves very slowly through the soils, which gives it a lot of time to lose the atmospheric oxygen it accumulated as it fell to earth. Since most plants need to have oxygen available to their roots, soils that stay wet for long periods, particularly during critical periods early in the growing season, exclude many species of plants. The levels of oxygen in these anaerobic soils are too low for most plants.

Upland areas are dominated by drought-tolerant plants, whose roots must be well aerated. These communities contain mostly scattered oaks and pines, which typically cover a low layer of shrubs, most of which are huckleberries. In contrast, wetlands contain plants that are sensitive to drought but can tolerate anaerobic soils. Forests in these areas contain two types of communities. The most unusual are stands of Atlantic white cedar. In these dark, densely packed stands, shrubs are relatively rare because the canopy both blocks light and filters out the wavelengths that most plants use in photosynthesis. Atlantic white cedar may make up over 95 percent of the trees, and they often grow so closely together as to hinder walking. This is made even more difficult by the ground surface, which undulates markedly, alternating between hummocks, pools of water, and mud holes. Another wetland community often borders cedar swamps. These more complex areas contain stands comprised of three or four species of hardwoods and one or two of pines above a well-developed, often thick shrub layer that may include a half dozen common species.

Decomposition of plant debris is slow in wetland locations again because not much oxygen is present in the soils. The lack of oxygen decreases the efficiency with which bacteria and fungi break down the organic material. As a result, this material, particularly organic acids, tannins, and humus, accumulates. These compounds leach into the ground water, which carries them into streams and rivers, where they combine with iron to produce the reddish, tea-colored waters that are typical of the Pine Barrens. While streams and rivers are typically slow-moving in the Pinelands, water sometimes cascades over artificial structures like spill-ways. There, the organic materials that have leached out of swamps and bogs often create a foam that persists on the water's surface. People sometimes confuse this with pollution, particularly given New Jersey's reputation in this regard. However, the waters of the Pine Barrens are seldom polluted because they move through sterile sands, have low nutrient concentrations, and are acid (Patrick et al. 1979), which inhibits the growth of many species of bacteria, making the waters even more pure. Rather than being polluted, the waters of the Pine Barrens are one of its greatest resources and one of the rationales the Pinelands Commission uses to protect this distinctive area.

The unusual conditions of the Pine Barrens—the sandy, acid soils; the large areas of wetlands; the great expanse of forests; and the frequent fires—create an area that is ecologically distinctive. The Pine Barrens are home to a few species that are found nowhere else on the planet. Other species are found in only a few areas outside the Pine Barrens. Of all the plants in the Pine Barrens, fully 8 percent are listed as rare, threatened, or endangered; this is a level that is two times that found in the rest of the continental United States (Fairbrothers 1979). The picture for amphibians and reptiles is similar (Conant 1979). The presence of unusual ecological conditions and the high percentage of rare species are the second reason the Pine Barrens are protected.

You might think this area is pristine and untouched by humans. However, the vegetation and ecology of the Pine Barrens are very much the result of human activity. People have been altering the Pinelands even before the coming of Europeans. Early explorers commented about the burning of the Barrens by Native Americans as they changed the forest to encourage species of plants and animals that were useful as food (Little 1979). While the area was neither quickly settled nor densely occupied, European colonists cut and burned the forests many times over as they exploited the area for wood. At first, Atlantic white cedar and large pines were cut for lumber. The cedar were valued for roofing since they are light, easy to work, and easy to wet down in case of fire. After those resources were depleted, pines were used for charcoal (Wacker 1979).

The area had a combination of raw materials and waterways for both transportation and energy. Wood was made into charcoal, which was burned to refine iron, using the area's low-grade iron ore and mollusk shells from the nearby ocean. The area contained sand for glass making, and clay deposits for brick and pottery manufacture. Paper milling, another local industry, relied mostly on salt marsh grasses. At one time, the area was a center for manufacturing (Wacker 1979). However, it was sparsely settled for several reasons. The area's agricultural and forest productivity was low. Settlements had to be scattered because of the extensive areas of forest that were needed to produce enough charcoal to supply local industry. Because villages were small and scattered, the style of manufacturing that was practiced here was much like plantation agriculture, with workers imported from outside the area contracting for long periods of employment while they lived in small factory towns. These towns were largely independent in terms of food and contained both grist and lumber mills, company stores, and surrounding cropland. Dependence on a renewable supply of wood was critical (Berger and Sinton 1985).

By the late 1800s these industries disappeared as the pine woods were depleted over and over again. In addition, better methods of transportation and higher-quality ores in other areas meant that resources could be easily transported to cities, with their ready supply of labor and access to markets (Berger and Sinton 1985; Collins et al. 1988). Places like Harrisville, Martha's Furnace, Washington Forge, and Weymouth are little more than ruins today. Batsto, on Burlington County Route 542, offers the best preserved example of that lifestyle, but even there, the iron smelting furnace is gone, as is the glassworks. Nearby Pleasant Mills exemplifies an early paper mill. More commonly, the only reminders of a lifestyle long past are the scattered ponds that once powered mills throughout the Pines (Collins et al. 1988). In some areas, you can see the remnants of roads and canals that transected this area. Most of the wood-framed buildings were destroyed by the forest fires so common to the region. The pine woods have now reclaimed many of the places where towns once stood, leaving only scattered cellar holes and small stands of non-native plants to remind us of their passing. West of Bass River State Forest, a collection of shagbark hickory (*Carya ovata*), with its distinctive bark that peels off in long vertical strips, stands along depressions to mark one such village.

The people who have remained live as Pineys always have, mostly by raising a few crops, by taking game and other resources from the woods, and by harvesting the nearby bays. Today, many work in nearby towns or for the state in Pinelands parks and forests, but their lives are paced by the traditions of living in the Pines that go back through families sometimes for hundreds of years. Some newcomers accept this lifestyle and absorb the culture. More frequently now, many people live within the Pines without really becoming part of the Pines.

Like the ecology of this quiet and sometimes seemingly desolate area, the culture is also vulnerable. Both ecologies and cultures change over time, but the pace of change and the extent to which new people move into an area determines whether the ecology and the culture will evolve slowly or whether they will suffer irreparable loss. The Pinelands has attracted development and speculation literally for hundreds of years. Even before Joseph Wharton consolidated his purchase of over 100,000 acres of land in the late 1800s, virtually all of the land of the Pine Barrens was owned by absentee landlords, who could neither control their holdings nor wrest much profit from them (Berger and Sinton 1985; McCormick 1979). People who lived in the Pine Barrens became accustomed to the fact that almost all of the land was owned by outsiders. By the time Wharton purchased his tract, land could be bought for relatively little because the woods had been depleted of useful lumber.

However, Wharton had another scheme. He saw the possibility of sending water from this area to Philadelphia, which was in the middle of a crisis over potable water, fueled in part by the health community's realization of the relationship between pollution and water-borne disease. His plan was circumvented by an act of the New Jersey legislature in 1884 (Berger and Sinton 1985), and his heirs eventually sold this large expanse of land in the central Pine Barrens to the state of New Jersey.

Since the area was first discovered by Europeans, speculators have seen opportunities for other sorts of development in the Pinelands. While cities like Hammonton and Egg Harbor City were developed to bring immigrants into the area for farming and industry, other schemes had a less noble basis. The most notorious of these was Paisley Village, which was a scheme to sell land in a city that existed mostly on paper and in the imaginations of those interested in relocating to the Pines (Berger and Sinton 1985). Even today, many townships in the Pine Barrens are broken up into small, sometimes miniscule lots on streets the township owns but will never, and likely can never, develop. These lots and "paper streets" exist only on the township's official maps. Most of these lots are the land that was once sold along with promises of new cities and increasing land values. In some cases, lots were given away as door prizes in burlesque halls and movie theaters. Now, many have reverted to the local townships when their owners tired of paying taxes on land that had no commercial value.

These earlier efforts to develop areas of the Pine Barrens pale beside more recent proposals, which have included plans to build a giant airport serving New York and Philadelphia and a place called "New City," which was supposed to house one-quarter of a million people. While these ideas were wildly impractical, more diffuse development has progressed at an increasing pace, such that during the 1960s and 1970s, townships within the Pine Barrens were among the fastest-growing areas of the nation (Collins 1988).

A consortium of environmental groups, concerned over the effect continued growth would have on the water, ecology, culture, and recreational resources of the Pinelands, mobilized to try to protect the Pine Barrens. These efforts were countered by those of organizations representing the interests of builders and real estate developers. The two factions wrestled first over how best to protect their conflicting interests and then whether to protect the Pines during a twenty-year period that culminated in the creation of the Pinelands Commission in 1979 and the Comprehensive Management Plan in 1980. These are the result of both federal and state legislation directed toward protecting the more than a million acres that are now the country's first National Reserve (Collins 1988; Russell 1988).

The reactions of locals to the Pinelands Commission mostly mimic the interests that fought, and continue to fight, over the Pinelands. Some object to what they perceive as governmental control that limits what individuals can do with their land. Others see the Commission as an important ally, protecting the rural character of their communities. Sometimes, the reactions of locals is downright curious, as when some alternate between being protectionist at one local meeting and libertarian at the next, depending on how they perceive their immediate interests.

What is clear is that population pressures have not abated since the adoption of the Pinelands Comprehensive Management Plan (CMP) in 1980. By law this plan must be periodically reviewed and possibly modified. While it is safe to say that the ecological, cultural, and hydrological resources of the Pines seem secure right now, this is the largest area of undeveloped land in the Northeast Corridor and a substantial economic attraction. The Comprehensive Management Plan could become weakened in the interest of development. Because of that, the Pine Barrens are, and will continue to be, endangered, particularly as the magnitude and pace of change today is very different from what the Pinelands experienced in the past. I cannot say whether our children will return to the Pines to find essentially what we see today. Given the sweep of the Pinelands Commission's charge, that seems likely. However, the issue was in doubt twenty years ago. Twenty years hence, who is to say?

Chapter 2

The Basic Features of Woody Plants

When I was a boy, I spent a considerable amount of vacation time with Stanley Smith, a botanist working at the New York State Museum in Albany. This brilliant man had the patience to introduce an inexperienced but eager young person to field biology and botany. Dr. Smith once told me something about the organisms of the natural world, something that has stayed with me. "Sometimes," he said, "these plants just don't read the same books we do."

His point was that things are often not as simple as they are portrayed in textbooks, nor as easy as we would prefer. The natural world and the organisms that inhabit it are incredibly varied, and the explanations of textbooks and field guides cannot cover all of these possible variations. Sometimes, things just do not follow the patterns we think they do. Sometimes, the distinctions we make do not work. I call this idea "Smith's principle" in honor of this fine, patient man. As you begin to learn the features of woody plants, keep it in mind. I will try to reduce ambiguity as much as possible and make learning the features of woody plants as easy as I can. However, all organisms show variation owing to differences in their genetics and the local ecology. In woody plants, there is often additional variation between parts, based on their location on the plant. For example, leaves vary depending on position and the amount of available sunlight. Also, twigs, branches, buds, and leaf scars all will vary considerably, based on whether they come from a new twig or an old branch.

Woody plants (those with a woody stem) grow from buds or tissue that is located on the branches. Much of this growth occurs near the tips of these branches and well above ground. Unlike herbaceous, i.e., nonwoody plants, the woody tissue supporting the leaves survives over winter, and more is added each year as the plant grows. So every year, twigs (new growth for that season) are added to branches (the growth of previous years). Each year, the new growth is added at the buds (Fig. 6). Having a woody stem that persists over winter and that grows year after year creates a structure that keeps a plant's leaves high in the air. This brings them closer to better-quality light, which plants convert into food via photosynthesis. Woody plants use this approach to out-compete nonwoody plants.

However, this strategy has its downside because woody tissue is harder to make than softer, herbaceous tissue. As a result, growth in woody plants is slower. Where rapid growth is an advantage (in open areas, for example), herbaceous plants often out-compete woody plants.

There are several basic features that are used to place woody plants in subcategories that make identification easier. These include the basic leaf type, branching pattern, type of end buds, and type of fruit. Each of these is described below along with illustrations that show important features.

Botanists usually begin keys by dividing plants into two categories: those with needle-like, nail-like, or scale-like leaves versus those with broad leaves. Most of the former are plants whose seeds are not enclosed in a true fruit, which is a remnant of a portion of the flower. These nonflowering plants are gymnosperms, a group containing pines, cedars, and junipers. On the other hand, native broad-leaf plants of the Pine Barrens are angiosperms, plants that bear flowers and some kind of fruit at some point during their life cycle. In our area, there are also a few plants with needle-like, nail-like, or scalelike leaves that bear flowers and fruit. Pyxie moss (*Pyxidanthera barbulata,* Fig. 2) is one of these.

Many people call gymnosperms "evergreens" because in our area pines, cedars, and junipers keep their leaves all year round. However, some flowering plants are also evergreen because, like gymnosperms, they retain their leaves over winter. Many of these plants have broad leaves. In our area they include mountain laurel, sheep laurel, and hollies, all of which are evergreen but flower at some time during the year and therefore are not gymnosperms. In that respect, they are like cherries, blueberries, oaks, and maples.

The flowers of cherries and blueberries are obvious. Oaks, maples, birches, and many other plants have inconspicuous flowers because they do not need to attract insects to help them transfer pollen (Figs. 7 and 14, for example). Instead, they rely on the wind. Many people mistakenly think that plants with wind-borne pollen do not flower because their flowers are inconspicuous, but these are true flowering plants nonetheless. The grasses are a good example of a plant whose flower is highly modified for wind pollination. Of course, most grasses are nonwoody; bamboo is one exception.

Your first decision about a plant should be whether it has a broad leaf or whether it exhibits the alternative characteristic and has needle-like, nail-like, or scale-like leaves. Needle-like leaves are long, thin, and very narrow, that is, they are at least twenty times longer than wide (Fig. 3). Because these leaves are embedded in a short sheath near where they join the twig, they are tied together at the base. Thus, we say that these needle-like leaves are arranged in "bundles." Native pines have needle-like leaves arranged in bundles of three or, less commonly, two, but bundles of five are found in one introduced species. Nail-like leaves are shorter than needle-like leaves, typically less than ten times longer than their width (Fig. 4). They resemble slightly flattened spikes rather than long needles. More importantly, they are not arranged in bundles. The third type of leaf that is included within this group is scale-like. These are very small and flat, and they adhere to the twig along their entire margin, much like scales on a fish (Fig. 5).

Broad leaves are the typical flattened leaves with which you are undoubtedly familiar. They are much larger, thinner, and broader, with a larger surface area than the needle-like, nail-like, and scale-like leaves. Broad leaves come in a wide variety of shapes and arrangements, as will be discussed, and they are found on most of the woody plants of the Pine Barrens. Here, all these plants bear some sort of flower and fruit at some time during the growing season. Fruits may be fleshy berries (with or without a hard pit); hard, woody capsules; the winged "samara" of maple trees; nuts; and the grains of grasses, to name a few. Many of our common vegetables are really fruits, and these include tomatoes, squash, and cucumbers (but not potatoes, which are modified roots).

Your second decision is whether the branching pattern is alternate or opposite. Alternate branching is by far the most common. Leaves (and branches) arise from "nodes." The space between nodes is called the "internode" and is usually elongated (remember Smith's principle). In the winter, leaves are often missing, but they leave a leaf scar where the leaf has detached from the twig (Fig. 6). With alternate branching, there is one leaf (or leaf scar) per node. At the next node, there is another leaf emerging from the other side of the twig or branch. The leaf placement is a bit like the climbing spikes on an old-fashioned telephone pole, with one on one side alternating with the next on the other.

With opposite branching, there are two leaves, or leaf scars, per node. These are opposite each other. If the plant has more than two leaves or leaf scars per node it is said to have a whorled branching pattern. If you identify a plant that has leaves or leaf scars arranged in whorls, key it out as a plant with opposite branching. Figure 7 illustrates opposite branching.

Sometimes plants with an alternate pattern of branching appear to have an opposite branching pattern because the space between the nodes is so small. As a result, the leaves are all bunched together, making the branching pattern appear opposite or whorled on first examination. In several species, the growth gets compressed, or crowded, near the tip, although farther down the branch it is typically more spread out. How do you determine whether a plant that grows like this really has alternate branching? Simple. Look at older branches or lower down on the twig. If the plant really has opposite branching, virtually all of its leaf scars will be opposite each other. If the young branches look opposite, but the leaves or leaf scars someplace else show an alternating pattern, the plant actually has alternate branching. This is yet another reason for picking a large sample to examine. With only a short twig, you might very well confuse alternate branching with opposite branching. The azaleas have alternate branching that sometimes looks opposite because their growth is often compressed near the tip of the twig (Fig. 8).

Opposite branching can also resemble alternate branching, of course. In maples and other plants with opposite branching, twigs might break off so that only one seems to arise from a node. This pattern is easy to identify correctly. Just look at a lot of branches and twigs. The opposite branching pattern should be clear once you examine the nodes to see whether there is one or two or more leaves, or leaf scars, per node.

To make identification easier, we divide broad-leaf plants into two categories: those with simple leaves and those with compound leaves. Simple leaves have one leaf blade on the leaf stem (the petiole). The plants in Figures 8 and 9 show simple leaves.

In compound leaves, the leaf blade is broken up into separate leaflets, which typically look like miniature leaves (Fig. 10). The leaflets are arranged in one of two patterns, depending on the species. In one pattern, the leaflets form two rows, one on each side of the leaf stem. The vein of each leaflet attaches to the side of the central stem, and that central stem eventually attaches to the woody twig or branch. This pattern is called "pinnate," but I will refer to it as "leaflets in rows." The sumacs and roses (Figs. 10 and 11) both show this pattern, as do the walnuts and hickories.

In the other pattern, the leaflets radiate out from the end of the stem, very much like your fingers radiate out from the palm of your hand. Therefore, the pattern is called "palmate." The main veins of all the leaflets meet at one point, where the leaf stalk connects to the woody portion of the plant (Fig. 12). When the leaf blade has only three leaflets, it has neither pattern, i.e., neither palmate nor leaflets in rows. Poison ivy (Fig. 1) shows this leaf type.

How do you tell a compound leaf from a simple leaf? One of the ways you can tell a compound leaf that has a series of leaflets from a twig that has a series of leaves is that in the case of the compound leaf, the leaflets attach to a fleshy stem and not a woody twig. Simple leaves, on the other hand, attach to a woody twig or branch. A second way to identify compound leaves is by looking to see where the bud is located. Most woody plants have a bud located on the twig above the leaf stem. These are called lateral buds. Buds are never found above the leaflets of a compound leaf. They are located at the base of the stem and on woody tissue (the twig or branch). Finally, you can sometimes remove a leaf by putting pressure on the top of the stem where it joins the woody twig or branch. When the leaf drops off, it leaves a leaf scar. The leaflets of a compound leaf seldom break off like this. A compound leaf typically falls off as a whole, with the leaflets attached. On the other hand, sometimes the leaflets drop off first, another example of Smith's principle. Table 2.1 summarizes the differences between simple and compound leaves.

Leaves show many different overall shapes, from round to elongate and everything in between, and there is an amazing variety in the shape of different parts, like the edges, the base, and the tip. The literature of botany is replete with terms that describe the many shapes of the whole leaf and specific parts.

Some leaves are lobed. Both sassafras and mulberries show this feature, as do many of the oaks. The edge of a lobed leaf is very wavy, cutting in toward the leaf stem and out again. Thus, the outer portion of the leaf is broken up by large cuts, or gaps, called "sinuses." For a leaf to be lobed, the sinus has to be deep. That is, the cut has to extend from the edge of the leaf at least one-third of the way into the blade toward the leaf stem.

Lobes are more apparent on some leaves than others. For example, in some species the leaves that are exposed to more light have deeper sinuses and therefore more pronounced lobes. In more extreme cases, some leaves are lobed while others on the same tree are not. *Sassafras* is notorious for having leaves of three different shapes on the same tree. These include nonlobed leaves, leaves that have two lobes and look like a mitten with a smaller "thumb" lobe, and leaves with one large central lobe and two smaller lateral lobes flanking it near the base of the leaf (Fig. 13). Mulberries (*Morus spp.*) are similar in this respect (Fig. 9).

Lobes of some plants show a palmate pattern (for example, the maples, Fig. 7). However, white oaks (*Quercus alba*) and scarlet oaks (*Q. coccinea*) have their lobes arranged in rows (Figs. 14 and 15).

Table 2.1. Comparing the Features of Simple and Compound Leaves

Feature	*Simple Leaf*	*Compound Leaf*
Leaf appears to attach to . . .	. . . a leaf stem that attaches to a woody twig.	. . . a fleshy, flexible stem. Blades of leaflets may attach directly to this fleshy stem, or they may attach to smaller stalks. In either case, the stems are soft and flexible. To put it another way, the woody twig has a thin, flexible leaf stem attached, with smaller leaflets attached to this nonwoody leaf stem.
Lateral buds are located . . .	. . . on the woody twigs and above where the leaf stem attaches to the woody twig. There is **one** leaf blade, though it may be lobed.	. . . also on the woody twig, though they may not be apparent in some species. The **important point** is that there are no lateral buds above the small leaflets of a compound leaf.
Pressing on the leaf stem . . .	. . . sometimes causes the single leaf to pop off, leaving a leaf scar marking the point of attachment.	. . . sometimes causes the collection of leaflets and flexible leaf stem to pop off, leaving a leaf scar behind.

To try to simplify the terminology, I have avoided most of the more complex terms describing leaf shapes. However, I have included a few that describe the tips and bases of leaves, which are illustrated in Figure 16 and in some of the subsequent figures.

The margins of leaves also vary, of course. Leaves of some species have smooth margins (also called entire leaves, Figs. 17, 18, 19, and 20), while in others they might be broken up into teeth, much like the cutting edge of a hand saw. Depending on the size, these are called serrations, dentations, or teeth. We will use the latter term and describe the size of the teeth as fine (Figs. 21 and 22) or coarse (Figs. 23 and 24). The leaves of sweet fern, *Comptonia peregrina* (Fig. 25), might be described as either coarsely toothed or lobed because the leaf is so narrow that the cuts between the teeth extend more than one-third of the way to the main vein.

It is hard to provide a value that separates fine teeth from coarse teeth.

Anything with a notch that is deeper than ½ inch qualifies as a coarse tooth. Anything less than ¼ inch should be considered a fine tooth. In the key, I try to provide a value for the depth of the notch in those borderline cases where I use the terms "fine" or "coarse" in my comparisons. Teeth can be found all along the edge of the leaf, as in the illustrations referred to above, or they can be limited to only a few near the tip of the leaf (Figs. 26 and 27). In a few cases, plants have double teeth, that is, they have fine teeth set on coarser teeth (Figs. 28 and 29).

Tiny hairs, or cilia, may also line the margin of the leaf. These look like teeth in a cursory examination, but under a hand lens the tiny hairs are evident. These may be found along the edges of leaves with smooth margins (Fig. 30) or at the tips of the teeth, in which case the tip is called "bristled" (Fig. 15).

Wherever a leaf drops off a branch, a leaf scar remains (Figs. 6 and 31). These, and the area around them, exhibit features that enable you to identify the plant. These features are particularly helpful in confirming identifications when the plant has its leaves. Over winter, these features become critical. Leaf scars vary in shape and are, like leaves, characteristic for a species. They may form thin crescents, or they might be shield-shaped, oval, round, or lobed. Plants on which the twigs grow very slowly often have leaf scars clustered together, while those with more rapid twig growth have leaf scars that are spread out along the twig. This pattern of growth varies depending on the species and may even vary with the location on the plant. Sometimes growth occurs more slowly toward the tip, where the leaf scars may be bunched so closely together as to make the branching pattern appear whorled, although farther down the alternate growth pattern is more apparent. In other species, growth may be so slow on some branches and twigs that the branches form short "spur branches." Apples, black gum, and a few other species have leaf scars bunched together and looking like rings.

Bundle scars are found within the leaf scar. These mark the place where the vascular bundle, or leaf vein, attaches to the twig or branch. Bundle scars appear as little dots, circles, or variously shaped lines within the leaf scar, and you will need to use a hand lens to see them (Figs. 6 and 31). Bundle scars can also be seen in other figures. In some species, bundle scars are more easily seen in older leaf scars, while in others, young leaf scars will show bundle scars more clearly. In a very few cases, you will have to carefully cut off the leaf to expose the bundle scars. If that is necessary, cut the leaf scar at the base, close to where it joins the twig or branch. Be careful not to cut off the bud because if you do, you may confuse that scar with another bundle scar.

The number of bundle scars is an important feature of plants. Many plants have only one bundle scar per leaf scar, which sometimes gives the leaf scar a "bull's eye" appearance, particularly if the leaf scar is round and the bundle scar is a dot. The bundle scar can be elongated into a line or a crescent shape as well. Other plants may have three bundle scars in a line or arc. A few plants have more than three bundle scars. Oaks illustrate this feature. Be careful to check several leaf scars before you decide how many bundle scars are present. Several plants, including apples, June (or service) berries, and roses, have the leaf scar elongated into a very narrow arch, which looks a little like a smile. These species have three bundle scars within an often narrow leaf scar. There is one bundle scar in the center but also one at each end. The latter two are very often missed by the novice because the leaf scar is so narrow.

In the following keys, the number of bundle scars is mentioned as a secondary feature to help you decide which of the two alternatives is correct. In these cases, be sure to examine leaf scars to see if the number of bundle scars is consistent with the primary trait. If it is not, you might want to reconsider your initial decision.

Some species produce *stipules*—small structures on the twig at the base of the leaf stem. Typically, they flank the leaf stem and are usually paired. Their shape varies enormously from extensions of the base of the leaf stem to triangular dots, small spikes or thorns, or things that look like small leaves. They may attach to the leaf stem and clasp, or they may be modified into long thread or stringlike *tendrils* (Fig. 33), which are used by climbing vines to grasp the branches of other plants. Stipules that attach to the leaf stem are usually green, like the leaves, while those that are free from the leaf stem may be more dark in color, usually darker than the twig. Figure 11 shows how the stipules of roses grow from the twig to the leaf stem. The stipules may be winglike on some roses, although in one species (*Rosa multiflora*) the stipules have tiny hairs lining their edges. The hollies (genus *Ilex*) are identified by small, dark-colored, triangular stipules that flank the base of the leaf stem. This feature is illustrated in Figure 27 for inkberry (*Ilex glabra*) and in Figures 31 and 33 for smooth winterberry (*Ilex laevigata*).

When the stipules drop off, they leave scars flanking either the base of the leaf stem or the edges of the leaf scar. In the hollies mentioned above, the stipule falls off to reveal a small, triangular, blackish scar (Figs. 27, 32, and 33). Other stipule scars may resemble lines and dashes (Fig. 6). In some cases, a stipule scar will encircle the twig, making a ring above or below the leaf scar (Figs. 17 and 18).

Buds are small bundles of tissue from which other structures later develop. They vary in shape, number, and placement. Some are inconspicuous (Figs. 10 and 11). Others may be clustered at the ends of the twigs. This feature is distinctive for the oaks (Fig. 13, shown enlarged in Fig. 34) and the wild azaleas (genus *Rhododendron,* Fig. 35). Most buds are covered by bud scales, which show characteristic numbers and patterns in certain species. There may be one bud scale that covers the whole bud more or less like a cap or hood pulled over a head (Fig. 36), or there may be several (for example, Figs. 6, 34, and 37). Occasionally, the arrangement of bud scales is particularly useful in identifying a certain species. While most plants have the scales clasping the sides of the bud, the poplars (*Populus spp.*) have the lowest bud scale clasping the front of the bud and thus, positioned right above the leaf scar (Fig. 38).

Flower buds develop into flowers, which in turn become fruit after the flower is pollinated and matures. These buds are usually larger than other buds (Fig. 35), or they may have a different appearance (Figs. 39 and 40). Depending on the plant, they can be arranged differently, sometimes in a kind of cluster or spike (Fig. 41).

New growth can arise from leaf buds, both lateral and terminal (or "end buds"). Each season, new woody growth forms a twig. After one season the twig becomes a branch, and a new twig grows from that branch during the growing season. Often, you can see where the new growth has begun because the twig and the young branch (the "branchlet" that was last season's twig) are of different colors or textures. In some species, there can be a line clearly separating the two (Figs. 5, 6, and 21).

Terminal buds are located at the very end, or tip, of the twig. Lateral buds are scattered along twigs and branches above the leaves or leaf scars (Figs. 6, 21, and 38, for example). Sometimes there is a bud at the very end of the twig, but it is not really a terminal bud even though it is located where a terminal bud would normally be found. This bud is called a "false end bud" (or "false terminal," or "pseudoterminal" bud). Because many species common to the Pine Barrens exhibit this feature, understanding the difference between true and false end buds is critical to correctly identifying these species.

There are several distinguishing features. First, a false terminal bud is usually angled slightly; that is, it does not grow straight beyond the twig the way a true terminal bud would. Second, while there will be a leaf scar below one side of both a true terminal bud and a false terminal bud, there should be a remnant of a stem opposite the leaf scar of a false terminal bud (Figs. 23, 37, and 42). This remnant may not be very large, but it usually extends a bit beyond the base of the false end bud. It may be nothing more than a small scar, but its presence indicates that you are actually looking at a false terminal bud. It has these features because it is really a lateral bud that used to have some structure beyond it. When that structure broke off, it left the lateral bud behind, but now located at the end of the twig in a position where you would normally find the true terminal bud.

A true terminal bud will not have this remnant of a twig opposite the leaf scar, and it will extend straight beyond the twig (Figs. 6, 43, and 44). Unfortunately, your terminal bud may have a second leaf scar opposite the first if the growth of the plant is crowded near the tip. If you find this is the case, verify that you are looking at two leaf scars by looking to see if the bud is angled or straight. See if the twigs grow such that their growth is crowded toward the tip. In addition, see if what you think might be a second leaf scar has all the features you expect to see in the leaf scar of that particular plant. If it looks more like a withered piece of stem and if it lacks all the features you find in other leaf scars, the bud is probably a false end bud. Of course, when in doubt, examine many samples. Figures 26, 28, and 38 show species that also have true end buds.

True fruit is found in flowering plants and is an enlarged remnant of the fertilized flower. Botanists have many terms for different types of fruit, and many of these are incorporated into the common language. Terms like "nut" and "berry" have specific meanings to botanists, meanings that are sometimes different from common usage. Other terms, like "pome," "achene," "samara," and "drupe," are not used in common speech. Pomes are compound fruits (that is, they grew from a flower's ovary that had many rows of seeds). More importantly, these have a papery husk inside, surrounding the seeds. Apples are a familiar example. Achenes are thin-walled fruits like the sunflower seed that contain only one seed within a husk. Samaras are winged fruits like those of the maple tree. Drupes include peaches and cherries, fleshy fruits in which the seed is surrounded by a stone.

To simplify things, I will use only a few terms to describe fruit in this key. For our purposes, berries are soft, fleshy fruits with small seeds (Figs. 31–33). Blueberries are a familiar example. If the fruit is a drupe, I will describe it as I have in the previous paragraph, i.e., berrylike with a stony pit.

Capsules are woody fruits that are often hard and closed when immature but that open spontaneously along several axes to shed seeds as they ripen. When ripe, they may be hard and resistant to pressure, or they may crumble easily. These fruits are usually found in clusters (Figs. 35 and 45–48). I will describe other fruits with short phrases so you can avoid learning a difficult vocabulary. Similarly, I will describe clusters of flowers using common speech to enable you to forgo learning the technical terms.

Pith is the tissue that runs through the middle of many twigs and branches. Typically, it is soft and spongy, and its color often differs slightly from that of the adjacent tissue. In some cases the color differences may be striking. Normally, pith is "continuous," that is, solid and not broken up into open and closed areas. If it is broken up in this manner, it is said to be "chambered" (Fig. 49). Pith may also be separated by small, woody partitions, in which case it is called "diaphragmed" (Fig. 50).

To look at the pith of a twig or branch, use a sharp knife, and gently whittle away the outer layers by slicing parallel to the twig. Take off thin slices so you avoid cutting through the pith. The idea is to expose a long portion of the center of the branch as cleanly as possible. If your knife is dull, it may squeeze portions of pith into little clumps, making what is really continuous pith appear to be chambered. Pith is usually round in cross section, but it can be triangular or even star-shaped in some species. To examine the shape of the pith in cross section, slice across the branch, but avoid compressing it. It might be more effective to slice at an angle using a whittling motion, although this will distort the shape of the pith slightly, making a round pith appear oval.

Chapter 3

How to Use a Dichotomous Key

Keys, more correctly called "dichotomous keys," are used by both students and professionals to identify unknown organisms. If we were making a choice among a few dozen plants, a simple list might suffice. You could read each description, compare it to your plant, and make a decision about whether your sample fits a description, in which case, you would have identified the species. If the two did not match, you would proceed to the next description. Eventually, you would find the best fit and the most likely identification of your sample.

However, it would be far too difficult to identify the plant if it meant that you had to read hundreds if not thousands of descriptions. The time and effort would be immense, and any mistake would be almost impossible to correct. Who could keep all the possible alternatives in mind if it meant he or she would have to wade through a score of possibilities, let alone over one hundred? Dichotomous keys are designed to circumvent this task and make the process of identification much more manageable.

A key works like a logic tree, in which you make a series of decisions about whether your unknown plant has (or does not have) certain features. At each numbered step in the key, you decide which alternative description, *a* or *b*, better fits your plant. Often, these alternatives are described in the form, *a* or *not a*. Each choice takes you to another pair of alternatives. You follow the directions for that pair, then the next, and so on until you have reached a correct identification. Often, the description will list more than one feature. In that case, rely more heavily on the initial ones because the features are listed either in order of importance, or in order of obviousness. Use the secondary features to confirm your decision.

Eventually, you will reach a point where the list of features describes your plant, and now you should have the name of a species. In some cases, the key will provide you with the name of the genus (for example, *Quercus spp.*, which means some species of *Quercus*, or an oak of some type). If your last feature just lists a genus, the key will refer you to another chapter, which will help you identify the correct species. There may even be a reference to an illustration that will help you confirm your identification.

Actually, knowing the genus of a plant is pretty good. In many cases, even experts who have devoted their lives to studying a group of plants will disagree on an identification of a species. Plants like roses, grapes, and blackberries confuse the best of us, and scientists often disagree on whether a variety constitutes a separate species or whether it is just a variant of another species.

A few points are worth repeating. When you key out a specimen, you go through a sequence of steps, each one of which is a simple choice as to whether your plant has (or does not have) certain features. Every time you make a choice, you narrow down the list by excluding species that lack the traits described at that decision point. After making that choice, you move to the next step, which presents another dichotomy. Do not proceed through the key sequentially from point 1 to point 2 to point 3. Follow the steps indicated by the key. If at step number 1 you select description *b* and that choice tells you to go to step number 122, you must skip steps 2 through 121. These are not relevant to your identification.

Also, read both descriptions fully to see which one seems to better fit your sample. Then read them each a second time, deciding whether your specimen is more accurately described in the first or second list. Your specimen might not have all the features listed. Choose the description that matches more closely.

Let us take a silly example to illustrate how dichotomous keys work. I might create a dichotomous key to my family. If you were presented with a member of my family, you could use this key to find out who this person is. For illustrative purposes I have omitted items 2 through 122.

1a. Younger than seventy. Go to 2.

1b. Older than seventy. Go to 123.

. . . .

123a. Male, balding or with gray hair; hair, if present, typically short; usually needs a shave; usually overweight. Go to 124.

123b. Female, gray-haired and not balding; hair longer than 3 inches in length; not known to shave; rarely overweight. Go to 135.

124a. Blue eyes, light hair, thick glasses. Father (Louis)

124b. Dark eyes, dark hair or if light then gray, glasses or not. (Uncles) Go to 125.

First, make a decision about the age of the person. Let us assume the person before you is older than age seventy. Skip items 2 through 122 since that includes children, brothers, sisters, cousins, nephews, and nieces. Go to item 123 and decide which alternative better describes the person before you. The most important item in this dichotomous choice is sex. The other features are less reliable. If you decide that the person before you is male, proceed to item 124. If the person before you has blue eyes, you have met my father, Louis. His eye color is unlikely to change. A few uncles have light hair that might be confused with my father's. Furthermore, my father might not be wearing glasses when you meet him. Rely more heavily on the initial features of the description.

Unfortunately, this example is simpler than those you might encounter once you start keying out plants. At some point, you may have a difficult time deciding whether the sample is better described by item *a* or *b* in the key. The best thing to do then is to make a note of that item number. Take your best guess and follow that path in the key. If you were correct, you should reach a point where the written description accurately fits your sample. If it does not, you have likely made a mistake, and you should go back to the point where you had trouble. Follow the other path (that is, select *b* instead of *a*), and proceed along that route. At some point, you should reach the name of a species and a description that fits the plant in several respects.

Some plants may or may not always show a certain feature. For example, both sassafras (*Sassafras albidum*) and red mulberry (*Morus rubra*) can have some leaves that are lobed and others that are not lobed. Whether the leaves are lobed depends on the genetic makeup of the individual plant and even the location on the plant. In the case of lobes, leaves that are higher on the plant are more likely to have lobes, and typically these are more pronounced on the higher leaves. To help you identify the plants of the Pine Barrens, I have included some species in more than one key when a feature is ambiguous or when a plant may or may not show it. That way, you will be able to key it out whichever route you take at the ambiguous feature.

When you are beginning to use any key, always start by identifying some species that you already know. That way, you will get a feel for how the key works.

Chapter 4

A Key to the Keys

Start with the key below to determine which of the subsequent keys to use to identify your plant.

1a. Plants with needlelike, nail-like, or scalelike leaves. Go to ke

Plants with needlelike, nail-like, or scalelike leaves retain most of their leaves over winter. Use key A to identify these plants year-round. Plants with the alternative trait (broad-leaved plants) typically lose their leaves in the fall, but some retain their leaves. For broad-leaved plants, use the key that is appropriate for the season.

1b. Leaves not as described above, or leaves absent. Go to 2.

2a. The plant is being identified during the growing season (spring, summer, and early autumn). Go to 5.

2b. The plant is being identified during the winter. Go to 3.

3a. Overwintering plants have at least some green leaves. Go to key E, chapter 5.

3b. Overwintering plants lack green leaves. Go to 4.

4a. Leaf scars opposite. Go to key F, chapter 5.

4b. Leaf scars alternate. Go to key G, chapter 5.

5. Plants identified during the growing season.

5a. Leaves and leaf scars opposite. Go to key B, chapter 5.

5b. Leaves and leaf scars alternate. Go to 6.

6a. Leaves compound; no buds at the bases of leaflets; buds, if present, are at the base of the flexible leaf stem and on a woody twig or branch. Go to key C, chapter 5.

6b. Leaves simple; leaflets lacking, although lobes may be present. Go to key D, chapter 5.

Chapter 5

Summer Keys to Most Species

A. Plants with Needlelike, Nail-like, or Scalelike Leaves

1a. Plants with either nail-like leaves, that is, shorter and thicker than needles, described below, and about twenty times longer than wide OR leaves that clasp the twig to form overlapping scales; leaves not bundled together in clumps, as described below. Go to 5.

1b. Plants with needlelike leaves, that is, much longer than wide (at least fifty times longer than wide); leaves bundled together in twos, threes, or fives; trees, saplings or shrubs (young saplings). *Pinus spp.*, pines (Fig. 3). Go to 2.

2a. Plants with leaves bundled together in units of five; leaves thin and not twisted; branches arise from each node in a whorl. Shape of tree symmetrical; bark smooth or with deep furrows; small branches not arising from thick blocky bark; long cones with scales that lack prickles. A non-native species that is common in some areas, particularly around houses or parks. *Pinus strobus*, white pine.

2b. Plants with leaves bundled together in units of two or three; leaves thicker and often twisted; shape of tree often asymmetrical; bark blocky and thick; small branches with needles occasionally arising from the bark, giving the tree a somewhat shaggy appearance; rounder cones with prickly scales. “Pitch pines” (Fig. 3). Go to 3.

3a. Cones with short, weak prickles; plants with needles, usually in bundles of two but sometimes in threes; needles bluish green, slender, not very twisted; bark blocky. *Pinus echinata*, shortleaf pine.

3b. Cones with sharp prickles. Go to 4.

4a. Plants with needles in bundles of three; needles yellowish green, twisted, stout, and 3–6 inches long; bark blocky with outer portions easily breaking off; cones with stout, sharp prickles on scales. *Pinus rigida*, pitch pine (Fig. 3).

4b. Plants with needles typically in bundles of two, 1½–3 inches long; cones with stout, sharp prickles on scales; bark blocky. *Pinus virginiana,* scrub or Jersey pine.

Note: There are two other species of pine that are found along the southwestern edge of the Pine Barrens. Both have needles bundled in twos and threes, but the needles are 5 to 10-plus inches long. *Pinus serotina,* the swamp pine, either has weak prickles, or it lacks prickles on its cones, which are typically under 2½ inches long. *Pinus taeda,* the loblolly pine, has stout, sharp prickles on cones that are typically longer than 2½ inches.

5a. Small, low shrubs with nail-like leaves; each leaf is long and attached to the twig at the narrow end. Go to 7.

5b. Trees, saplings, or tall shrubs with very small, scalelike leaves, although a few nail-like leaves may also be present; the scalelike leaves clasp the twig and overlap, giving the entire twig a scaly appearance. You might think that this green, scale-covered twig is a leaf, but in reality, you are looking at flattened leaves that adhere to the twigs. These are called "cedars" in southern New Jersey. Go to 6.

6a. Plant with twigs that are roughly square in cross section and NOT flattened; leaves often of two kinds, both scalelike that clasp the twig and nail-like that attach only by a narrow base and extend away from the twig. These plants reproduce via a hard, dark or green "berry." This small tree is commonly found in uplands and old fields. *Juniperus virginiana,* red cedar (Fig. 5).

6b. Plant with twigs that form slightly flattened sprays; only scalelike leaves present; cones are small, globular, and woody when mature. This thin, straight tree is limited to very wet areas, where it forms dense stands, often in standing water. *Chamaecyparis thyoides,* Atlantic white cedar.

7a. Leaves appear to clasp the branches and are covered with minute downy or wooly hair. Older leaves persist on the stem, where they turn brown; this gives the stem a shaggy appearance. Plants grow together in clumps, but they stand above ground, usually under 1 foot in height, sometimes resembling a small bonsai tree. The slender leaves appear thicker at the base and lack a leaf stem. *Hudsonia spp.*, false heather (Fig. 4). Go to 9.

7b. Leaves do not seem to clasp the branches but stand free at almost a right angle. Older leaves fall off the branches. Plant runs along surface of the ground, often forming mats. Leaves thickest in the middle or near the tip with a distinct leaf stem. Go to 8.

8a. Leaves appear opposite, often in whorls of three or four. Leaves with minute teeth (use hand lens) and thicker in the middle; base of leaf more rounded; tip rounded or with small point. *Corema conradii*, broom crowberry.

8b. Leaves clearly alternate, lacking minute teeth and thicker toward the tip; leaf tapers gradually to a fine point (not rounded); base of leaf gradually tapers to the leaf stem. This mosslike plant is found in the Pygmy Pine plains and other very dry, sandy locations. *Pyxidantera barbulata*, pyxie moss (Fig. 2).

9a. Leaves surrounded by thick wooly hair and tightly pressed to stem. This plant is usually found closer to the coast or inland in disturbed areas. *Hudsonia tomentosa*, wooly *Hudsonia*.

9b. Leaves hairy, spread slightly from branch, and not tightly clasping stem. This species is the common *Hudsonia*, which is found in disturbed inland areas. *Hudsonia ericoides*, downy *Hudsonia* (Fig. 4).

B. Broad-Leaf Plants with Leaves and Leaf Scars Opposite

1a. Leaves simple. Go to 3.

1b. Leaves compound with leaflets in rows; lateral buds may be found on the woody twigs and branches at the base of the compound leaf, but there are no lateral buds at the base of the leaflet. Go to 2.

2a. Shrubs have a well-developed pith; no single end bud; leaf scars connected by a line. *Sambucus canadensis*, common elderberry.

2b. Branches lack a well-developed pith. Leaf scars not connected by a line; true end buds with two bud scales. This is an uncommon plant, more common in the northern Pine Barrens but rare elsewhere. *Fraxinus pennsylvanica*, green ash.

3a. Leaves lobed. Go to 4.

3b. Leaves not lobed. Go to 7.

4a. Undersides of leaves densely hairy, a shrub. *Viburnum acericoides*, maple-leaved arrowwood.

4b. Undersides of leaves not densely hairy, trees. *Acer spp.* Go to 5.

5a. Leaves with coarse teeth, each ending in a very sharp point or bristle tip; leaf stem secretes a milky juice. This is an escapee not native to the Pine Barrens. *Acer platanoides*, Norway maple.

5b. Leaves with fine teeth or double-toothed. Go to 6.

6a. Leaves usually have three prominent lobes but as many as five, in which case the lower two are poorly developed. Buds reddish. This tree is common in wet areas and when young has smooth, gray bark. *Acer rubrum*, red maple (Fig. 7).

6b. Leaves with five, seven, or nine lobes that are separated by deep sinuses, or cuts. This small tree is also not native to our area. *Acer plamatum,* Japanese maple.

7a. Plant upright, a tree or a shrub; some may be low shrubs. Go to 9.

7b. Plant is a low creeping shrub. These plants crawl along the surface of the ground, or they are vinelike and crawl over the ground, sometimes also climbing on other plants. Go to 8.

8a. Leaves less than 1 inch long with a rounded base. A small, green, barely woody, trailing shrub of wetlands. *Mitchella repens,* partridgeberry.

8b. Leaves typically longer than 2 inches; base of leaf tapers to the twig (leaf stem barely evident); twigs and leaves hairy. A common escapee that forms dense tangles, mostly running over the ground. Found in dryer locations. *Lonicera japonica,* Japanese honeysuckle.

9a. Leaves toothed, leaf bases rounded. Go to 10.

9b. Leaves not toothed, leaf bases rounded or not. Go to 12.

10a. Leaves coarse-toothed, with regularly spaced and sized teeth; buds with many scales; branches mostly straight and slender. *Viburnum dentatum,* arrowwood.

10b. Leaves fine-toothed. Go to 11.

11a. Terminal bud with only two scales; leaves sharply fine-toothed. *Viburnum prunifolium,* smooth blackhaw (Fig. 51).

11b. Terminal bud with two scales and a small portion of a third between them. This resembles a bird's head with two larger bud scales forming the upper and lower beaks and the smaller bud scale resembling an eye spot between them. *Viburnum nudum*, wild raisin (Fig. 39).

12a. Low shrubs with the largest leaves smaller than 2 inches long; leaves with semitransparent dots that let light pass through, or black dots (use hand lens); very small clusters of tiny leaves may be found at the base of the stems of the main leaves. *Hypericum spp.*, St. Johnsworts and St. Peterswort. See chapter 6.

12b. Transparent dots not present. Go to 13.

13a. Lateral leaf veins run to the edge of the leaf; or if they run along the edge, they break up into many smaller veins; or lateral leaf veins not evident. Go to 15.

13b. Lateral leaf veins run close to and parallel with the leaf edges. These veins do not break up as they parallel the edge of the leaf. See Figures 40 and 52. Go to 14.

14a. Leaves opposite and in pairs; twigs dark green to purple; end bud of two types, a flower bud that is rounded and on a stalk, and a vegetative bud that resembles the lateral buds (i.e., is elongate and not on a stalk). *Cornus florida*, flowering dogwood (Figs. 40 and 52).

14b. Leaves occasionally in whorls of three; twigs brown; lateral buds often hidden beneath the leaf stem; false end buds. A medium-sized or tall shrub with an unusual, round, hard fruit that is typically more than ½ inch in diameter. This plant is restricted to very moist areas, usually near water. *Cephalanthus occidentalis*, buttonbush.

15a. Buds mostly with two scales. The terminal bud sometimes resembles a bird's head with two larger bud scales and a smaller bud scale that resembles an eye spot between them. *Viburnum nudum,* wild raisin (Fig. 39).

15b. Buds mostly with more than two scales. Go to 16.

16a. Leaves mostly shorter than 5 inches and not usually heart-shaped. Go to 18.

The lilac, *Syringa vulgaris,* has short, heart-shaped leaves. It can be found in the wild around old house sites. Privet (see below) has some leaves with a heart-shaped base, although others are elliptical.

16b. Leaves mostly over 5 inches long and heart-shaped; trees; branches with well-developed pith. Go to 17.

17a. Leaves sometimes in whorls of three; pith solid and either white or very light; bark scaly; long, hard podlike fruit may be present; crushed leaves have an unpleasant smell. An introduced species more likely found around houses or in disturbed areas. *Catalpa speciosa,* catalpa or catawba.

N.B. Sandra Bierbrauer of Stockton College and Gerry Moore of the Brooklyn Botanic Garden believe that this species, rather than *Catalpa bignonoides,* is the common catalpa of the Pine Barrens. Moore indicated to me that both species can occur but that they can only be reliably differentiated by their flowers.

17b. Leaves never in whorls of three; pith chambered or hollow; fruits hard and nutlike; husks often remaining on tree; crushed leaves have no unpleasant odor; bark intermittently smooth and rough. Like the catalpa, another non-native species. *Paulownia tomentosa,* princess tree.

18a. Tall shrubs, over 3 feet; leaves usually with prominent lateral veins (except in Tartarian honeysuckle, which is readily identified by breaking open a young branch and looking for the hollow pith chamber). Go to 20.

18b. Small shrubs, under 3 feet; leaves have a prominent mid vein, but obscure lateral veins. Go to 19.

19a. Leaves typically less than 2 inches long and often in whorls of three; leaves light green and dull above; leaves persist over winter but are not particularly leathery; fruit a capsule. This plant often grows in clumps or small stands from an underground stem. *Kalmia angustifolia*, sheep laurel or sheepkill.

19b. Leaves small (under ½ inch long) and evergreen; leaves leathery, dark green, and shiny above; some leaves may be alternate. Shreddy bark. *Leiophyllum buxifolium*, sand myrtle.

20a. Leaves mostly elliptical, some may have a heart-shaped base; younger branches hollow; small, blunt buds with three or fewer bud scales; scales remain at the base of the twig and separate the year's growth from older growth; fruit a red (or sometimes yellow) berry. An introduced species. *Lonicera tatarica*, Tartarian honeysuckle.

20b. Leaves elliptical, never with a heart-shaped base; branches solid; scales separating the twigs from the branches do not persist. Go to 21.

21a. Leaves occasionally in whorls of three; leaf scars connected by a line; lateral buds often hidden beneath the leaf stem; false end buds. A medium-sized or tall shrub with an unusual, round, hard fruit that is usually more than ½ inch in diameter. This plant is restricted to very moist areas, typically near water. *Cephalanthus occidentalis*, buttonbush.

21b. Leaves never in whorls of three, lateral buds prominent, true end buds, leaf scars not connected by a line; fruit not a large, hard ball, but typically black when mature. Go to 22.

22a. Leaves mostly smaller than 2½ inches long, thin; leaf scar raised; twigs thinner than 1/16 inch in diameter. An escapee often found in disturbed areas. *Ligustrum vulgare*, common, or European, privet.

22b. Leaves mostly over 3 inches, some may be longer than 8 inches, slightly thickened; leaf scar not raised; twigs thicker than above. *Chionanthus virginicus*, fringe tree.

C. Broad-Leaf Plants with Alternate, Compound Leaves

Note: Poison ivy (item 8) and poison sumac (item 15) are included in this key. Both plants contain irritants. Go through the key being careful not to touch plants until you have ruled out these two species.

1a. Plants with thorns or prickles. Go to 2.

1b. Plants without thorns or prickles. Go to 7.

2a. Erect trees or shrubs; no arching, climbing, or running brambles. Go to 4.

2b. Arching, climbing, or running brambles; often forming dense thickets. Branches and twigs green or purple. Go to 3.

3a. Leaf scars very narrow and extending about halfway around the twig; base of leaf stem widens to form a leafy stipule that attaches to the twig; compound leaves have leaflets in rows. *Rosa spp.*, the roses. See chapter 6.

3b. Leaf scars not narrow and extending around the twig; no leafy stipule; leaves with three to five leaflets arranged in a palmate pattern. *Rubus spp.*, blackberries, dewberries. See chapter 6.

4a. Leaves compound; thorns paired at the base of the leaf stem. *Robinia spp.*, locusts. Go to 5.

4b. Some leaves twice compound (that is, leaflets themselves compound and broken down into subleaflets); thorns long, sometimes longer than 1 inch; some thorns branched; lateral buds surrounded by the base of the leaf stem or the leaf scar. *Gleditsia triacanthos*, honey locust.

5a. Shrubs; twigs and branches bristly. *Robinia hispida*, bristly locust or rose acacia.

5b. Trees and saplings; twigs and branches not bristly. Go to 6.

6a. Thorns well developed; leaflets mostly rounded at base and tip; twigs hairless and smooth. *Robinia psuedo-acacia*, black locust.

6b. Thorns weak, small (¼ inch or smaller); leaflets usually with a small point formed by the main vein extending beyond the leaf margin; twigs hairy with small glands. *Robinia viscosa*, clammy locust.

7. Plants without prickles or thorns.

7a. Erect trees or shrubs. Go to 10.

7b. Climbing vines. Go to 8.

8a. Leaflets three, either smooth-edged or with a few scattered teeth; leaves often glossy; typically, a running or climbing vine with a hairy stem and sometimes white berries, although it may grow as a shrub in some locales. *Toxicodendron radicans*, poison ivy. A toxic plant. Do not touch. (Fig. 1).

8b. Leaflets more than three, either entire or toothed; stems not hairy. Go to 9.

9a. Leaves palmately compound, usually with five leaflets; margin of leaflets coarsely toothed; tendrils present. *Parthenocissus quinquefolia*, Virginia creeper (Fig. 12).

9b. Leaflets in rows, more than five, and without teeth; branches twisted and often climbing high; fruit a beanlike pod; clusters of showy, lilac flowers. A non-native species that was planted around dwellings and has escaped. *Wisteria frutescens*, American wisteria.

10a. Leaves twice compound (leaflets compound and broken down into subleaflets); many small leaflets, which may close when touched; bark thin and scaly, twigs reddish. Not native to the Pine Barrens. *Albizzia julibrissin*, mimosa or albizzia.

10b. Leaves simply compound (leaflets not broken down into subleaflets). Go to 11.

11a. Leaves very small (compound leaf usually less than 2 inches long, including leaf stem); both simple and compound leaves may be present, the latter with three leaflets; branches very slender, dark green, furrowed, arching, and graceful. A small shrub that often grows from a clump. Another species not native to our area. *Cystisus scoparius*, Scotch broom.

11b. All leaves compound, some with more than three leaflets; not a small, arching shrub. Go to 12.

12a. Leaves very large, with many leaflets (11–41); leaflets on short stalks; leaflets may have one or two pairs of teeth at the base; base of leaflet not tapering to the leaf stem; leaf scars large and shield-shaped with many bundle scars around the margin; buds wooly with brown hairs. A tree or sapling. Not native to the Pine Barrens. *Ailanthus altissima*, tree of heaven.

12b. Leaves smaller, with up to 25 leaflets; leaflet base tapers to leaf stem; leaflets either toothed along entire margin or smooth. Go to 13.

13a. True end buds that are large (¼ inch or longer); lateral buds are visible. Go to 16.

13b. False end buds that are very small (less than ⅛ inch long); lateral buds small and mostly hidden by the leaf stem or partly surrounded by the leaf scars. Go to 14.

14a. Leaflets toothed; twigs very hairy; fruit a dense and nearly solid, reddish and hairy cluster of small "berries." *Rhus typhina*, staghorn sumac.

14b. Leaflets with smooth margins (entire). Go to 15.

15a. Main vein of leaf with a "wing" or small, leafy ridge between leaflets; twigs covered with small, dense hairs; bark with short, raised streaks running across. A small shrub found in drier areas. *Rhus copallina*, winged sumac (Fig. 10).

15b. Main vein without wing; twigs smooth; leaf scars do not surround buds. A tall shrub of wet areas. *Toxicodendron vernix*, poison sumac, a plant similar to poison ivy with an even more potent irritant.

16a. Leaflets typically more than seven, often more than nine; terminal leaflet often missing, giving the compound leaf an even number of leaflets; pith chambered by woody partitions; three groups of bundle scars, often in a lobed leaf scar. *Juglans nigra*, black walnut (Fig. 49).

16b. Leaflets seven or fewer; terminal leaflet present, giving leaves an odd number of leaflets ranging from five to nine; pith white and not chambered. Many bundle scars but not in three groups. *Carya spp.*, hickories. Go to 17.

17. There are two common hickories in most of the Pine Barrens. These are keyed out below. Both have tightly furrowed bark. Others are found at the periphery of the Pine Barrens or in scattered locations near where they were planted by settlers. If your specimen does not closely correspond to the two species below, see chapter 6.

17a. Leaf undersides and twigs wooly, usually with seven to nine leaflets, and fragrant when crushed. End buds ⅜ inch or larger, twigs thick. *Carya tomentosa,* mockernut hickory.

17b. Undersides of leaves and twigs not wooly, although they may be finely hairy, especially when young; typically seven to nine leaflets. Leaves not fragrant when crushed. End buds small (less than ⅜ inch). Twigs slender. *Carya glabra,* pignut hickory.

D. Broad-Leaf Plants with Alternate Simple Leaves

1a. Upright trees or shrubs, or low plants, some of which form mats; no tendrils present. Go to 3.

1b. Vines that form tangles or that climb upwards on other plants; tendrils present opposite some leaves. Go to 2.

2a. Plants with thorns; leaves with smooth margins; stems green; hard berries may be present; may form dense tangles. *Smilax spp.*, greenbriers (Fig. 32). See chapter 6.

2b. Plants without thorns; leaves lobed; stems brown; rarely forms dense tangles but rather, climbs upward, often into the tree canopy. *Vitis spp.*, wild grapes. See chapter 6.

3a. Plants taller than 4 inches (and not as described in 3b), including small shrubs, usually over 8 inches tall, as well as the more typical taller shrubs, saplings, and trees. Go to 9.

Note: Seedlings of taller plants might be confused with the plants described in 3a. To eliminate confusion, look for taller specimens of the same species. If you cannot find these in the area and your plant matches the description in 3b, you are probably correct in placing it there.

3b. Plants low (usually less than 4 inches tall), either solitary and slightly herbaceous, joined by underground stems, or forming dense mats on the surface of the ground. Go to 4.

4a. Leaves may have fine teeth. Go to 6.

4b. Leaves fleshy and leathery with few, coarse teeth; leaves may look whorled; plants solitary, with fleshy stems, or in small clumps. Go to 5.

5a. Leaves with a distinctive whitish streak down the center. *Chimaphila maculata*, spotted wintergreen (Fig. 24).

5b. Leaves without this distinctive whitish streak. *Chimaphila umbellata*, princess pine.

6a. Crushed leaves have a pleasant, spicy scent (like wintergreen or teaberry gum); individual plants connected by underground stems, growing in loose groups; leaves small, thick, evergreen, leathery, and nearly round. Red berries are white inside and taste like teaberry but are often mealy. *Gaultheria procumbens*, wintergreen or teaberry.

6b. Crushed leaves have no odor of winterberry or teaberry; red berries inedible or very sour; plants usually grow in dense clusters. Go to 7.

7a. Leaves large, 1–3 inches long, hairy beneath and sometimes above, often with a hairy fringe; leaves almost round with a long, hairy leaf stem; twigs hairy. *Epigaea repens,* trailing arbutus or mayflower.

7b. Leaves smaller, about 1 inch long, and oval or spatula-shaped; leaf stems, twigs, and edges of leaves not hairy as described above. Go to 8.

8a. A plant of wetlands and wet depressions; twigs hairless, leaves slightly whitened below and averaging about ½ inch in length; widest point of leaf about halfway from base to tip. Sour, red berries may be present; these lack a stony pit. *Vaccinium macrocarpon,* cranberry.

8b. A plant of dry uplands; twigs typically hairy, bark shreddy, leaves NOT slightly whitened below; leaves averaging about 1 inch in length, with widest point closer to base; fruit a small, dry red berry with a stony pit. *Arctostaphylos uva-ursi,* evergreen bearberry.

9. All of the following plants are upright shrubs or trees. They are not vines, low sprawling shrubs, or very low herblike plants.

9a. Twigs and young branches always speckled with many very tiny whitish dots (use a hand lens); twigs green, sometimes with red along one side. The tiny white dots found in this genus look like little pimples or tiny warts that densely cover the twigs and young branches. Do not confuse these many tiny white dots with larger, raised, darker spots, (lenticels). The latter are fewer in number and scattered along the twig.
Vaccinium spp., the blueberries (Figs. 37 and 53). See chapter 6.

9b. Twigs not speckled with many tiny white dots; lenticels, larger dots, or speckles may be present (if so, these are neither numerous, tiny, nor white); twigs of any color. Go to 10.

10a. Resin dots present on lower surface of leaves and sometimes on the upper surface, stems, and buds. Go to 11.

Use a hand lens to see resin dots, which are small, yellow globules that catch and reflect light like tiny droplets of pitch or resin. To see these, bend the leaf around your finger so you can see the underside and hold it to the light. By looking at the curved underside of the leaf, you will more easily see the light reflecting off the resin dots, which will look like tiny, jewel-like droplets in a strong light. They may look like yellow dots in weaker light.

10b. Resin dots not present on upper or lower surfaces of leaves; small brown dots or rusty scales may be present. These do not catch the light as described above. Go to 14.

11a. Crushed leaves have pleasant, spicy odor; three bundle scars. Go to 12.

11b. Crushed leaves have no pleasant, spicy odor; one bundle scar; leaves elliptical, edges smooth or toothed; if toothed, teeth extend along entire margin; tip of leaf rounded, often ending with one small projection of the main vein past the rounded tip; fruit a dark berry.
Gaylussacia spp., huckleberries (Figs. 42 and 54). See chapter 6.

12a. Leaves much longer than wide (about five to ten times longer than wide) with 12 to 20 distinctive rounded lobes, giving the leaf a wavy-edged appearance; each lobe may end in a slight point. Note the fernlike appearance of this small shrub, which has false but swollen end buds; twigs green and soft, with small buds at the base of the leaf stem. *Comptonia peregrina*, sweet fern (Fig. 25).

12b. Leaves not long and narrow, not lobed but smooth-edged, although a few teeth may be present toward the tip; small hard, waxy, light-colored berries may be present in clusters near leaf base; end buds true, buds light-colored. *Myrica spp.* (Fig. 27). Go to 13.

13a. Density of resin dots on upper surface of leaves is about half that of underside; leaves up to 4 or more inches long and up to ½ inch wide; undersides of leaves hairy; twigs hairy. This is the more common species. *Myrica penyslvanica,* bayberry.

13b. Density of resin dots is about the same on upper surface and underside of leaves; leaves 2–3 inches long and under ½ inch wide; undersides mostly hairless; twigs mostly hairless; less common and mostly along coastal areas. *Myrica cerifera,* wax myrtle.

14a. End buds clustered on tips of twigs; there may be one or a few large buds clustered together (Fig. 34), or there may be a single very large bud with smaller buds around its base (Fig. 35). This group includes the oaks, which may have branches too high to reach. In that case either look for typical lobed or toothed oak leaves or try to find acorns, either on the tree or on the ground under the tree. Do not confuse clusters of flower buds on a stalk (for example, Fig. 41) with end buds. Look for clusters of buds at the ends of the twigs. Go to 15.

14b. End buds not clustered at tips of twigs; single end buds (if present). Go to 18.

15a. Leaves with three (or, rarely, five) lobes that look somewhat like maple leaves; lobes are lined with rounded teeth; buds are very small and clustered at the ends of the twigs, which are often expanded; small, pointed stipules usually flank the base of the leaf stalk; a shrub; fruit a capsule; a plant not native to the Pine Barrens. *Hibiscus syriacus,* rose of Sharon.

15b. Leaves may be lobed or not, but if lobed, then without rounded teeth (rounded teeth may be present, but the leaf will have lobes in rows, not like a maple leaf); no stipules; tip of twig not expanded and has larger buds (at least one more than ¼ inch long). Go to 16.

16a. One bundle scar per leaf scar; edge of leaf is smooth, with many tiny hairs along edge (Fig. 30); one large and many small buds clustered on the tips of the twigs is the usual pattern; leaves often appear clustered at ends of slender twigs; twigs may also appear to be whorled at the ends of branches; fruit a capsule about ½ inch long. A tall shrub of wet areas. *Rhododendron spp.*, azaleas (Figs. 8, 30, and 35). Go to 17.

16b. Many bundle scars per leaf scar; leaves do not have tiny hairs along the margins, although a few bristle tips may be present; several large and smaller buds clustered on the tips of the twigs is the usual pattern; leaves are either lobed, have coarse teeth, or in one species are smooth-edged, long, and narrow (that is, about fifteen times longer than wide); leaves do not appear clustered at ends of slender twigs; acorns may be present. Trees or shrubs usually found in drier areas. *Quercus spp.*, the oaks. See chapter 6.

17a. Leaves shiny or glossy above, light-colored beneath; main vein is hairy on leaf underside; buds hairy; twigs hairy, sometimes densely hairy. *Rhododendron viscosum*, swamp azalea.

17b. Leaves dull above; midrib not hairy beneath; twigs and buds less hairy. *Rhododendron periclymenoides*, pink azalea.

Note: One species of *Rhododendron* can be found along the western edge of the Pine Barrens, although it is rare even there. This is *Rhododendron maximum*, the great laurel. Its leaves lack the many tiny hairs long their edges, but they are large, i.e., up to 7 inches long, and roughly oval in shape.

18a. Plant with two kinds of leaves; leaves on lower portion of plant are square or wedge-shaped with coarse teeth along the outer two edges (looking something like a folded fan); upper leaves elliptical with a pointed end and not toothed; three bundle scars; leaves densely covered with white dots; twigs green and angled from the branches; branches and stems have longitudinal grooves. A shrub mainly of coastal areas. *Baccharis halimifolia,* groundsel tree.

18b. Leaves on lower portion do not differ markedly from those on the upper portion, that is, they are not different in shape (fan-shaped versus elliptical); twigs not angled from the branches, although they may be green. Go to 19.

19a. Thorns present; these may be modified branches that end in a sharp point. Go to 20.

19b. Thorns not present; twigs do not end in a sharp point. Go to 22.

20a. Twigs, and often the undersides of the leaves, densely covered with silvery and rusty brown speckles or scales; these are visible to the naked eye; undersides of leaves have distinctly metallic silvery sheen; leaves elliptical and smoothed-edged or wavy. A small tree or tall shrub often found in old fields or along the sides of roads, and often growing in dense stands. *Elaeagnus umbellata,* autumn olive.

20b. Rusty brown and silvery scales described above are not found. Go to 21.

21a. False end buds; spines are modified branches and may have buds or leaves present; broken bark of twigs has an unpleasant “bitter almond” smell (cyanide); leaves mostly fine-toothed, each with a rounded base and distinct leaf stem. *Prunus americana,* American plum.

21b. True end buds; spines lack buds or leaves; broken bark does not smell of cyanide; leaves have coarse teeth (or double teeth), their stems short and gradually blending into their blades. *Crataegus uniflora,* dwarf hawthorn.

22a. Some or all leaves lobed. Go to 23.

22b. No lobed leaves present. Go to 28.

23a. Leaves symmetrical, with the number of lobes on one side equaling those on the other side; all leaves lobed. Go to 26.

23b. Some leaves irregularly lobed, that is, the number of lobes on one side is different from that on the other side. Both lobed leaves and nonlobed leaves may be present. Go to 24.

24a. Leaves have teeth. Crushed bark has no pleasant, spicy odor; leaves often irregularly lobed with two, three, or four lobes, or may have no lobes; leaf scars with many bundle scars; branches not greenish. *Morus spp.*, the mulberries (Fig. 9). Go to 25.

24b. Leaves lack teeth. Crushed bark of twigs has a pleasant, spicy odor; leaves may have two or three lobes, or may have no lobes; leaves with two lobes look like a mitten; leaves with three lobes are symmetrical, with the center lobe larger than the flanking lobes. All three types of leaves may be present on the same tree or sapling. Leaf scars with one elongate bundle scar; twigs and branches greenish. *Sassafras albidum,* sassafras (Figs. 13 and 55).

25a. Upper surface of leaves has a coarse, gritty feel; the dark red or purple "berries" are sweet; milky sap; a tree or shrub with false end buds; buds have five to six scales. *Morus rubra,* red mulberry.

25b. Upper surface of leaves does not have a coarse, gritty feel; white berries not sweet; sap not milky. *Morus alba,* white mulberry.

26a. Leaves with four symmetrical lobes, each of which ends in a point. The outline of the leaf resembles that of a tulip flower. Leafy stipules at base of leaf stem surround buds; buds with two scales.
Liriodendron tulipifera, tulip tree.

26b. Leaves with an odd number of lobes ranging, depending on the species, from three to seven. Go to 27.

27a. Star-shaped leaves with deep notches and fine teeth. Crushed leaves have a distinctive smell that some describe as pleasant while others find distasteful or "soapy." True terminal buds; buds with multiple scales; branches may have corky fins, or ridges, running along part of their length; bark evenly grooved and grayish. A woody, ball-like fruit studded with sharp teeth may be present.
Liquidambar styraciflua, sweet gum.

27b. Leaves with shallow lobes and few, coarse teeth; leaf base may surround lateral bud; end buds false; leafy stipules encircle the twigs at the bases of the leaves; stipule scars run around the branch in a line. Smooth bark peels off in large, irregular blocks; underbark yellowish, whitish. The distinctive bark with large white, yellowish, tan, and gray splotches makes this non-native tree easy to spot from long distances. *Platanus occidentalis*, sycamore.

28. Leaves not lobed.

28a. Stipule scar forms a line or ring around the twig where the leaf stem attaches to the twig; undersides of glossy, dark green leaves appear whitish; leaves large, some 4 or more inches long and with a smooth edge; crushed leaf has a pleasant, spicy smell; leaf scar has many bundle scars; the large end bud is covered by a single scale. A thin tree or sapling of wet areas. *Magnolia virginiana*, sweetbay magnolia (Figs. 17 and 18).

28b. Stipule scar that forms a ring around the twig where the leaf stem joins the twig is not present; leaf may be glossy but if so, the undersides are not whitish; leaf edge may be either smooth or toothed. Go to 29.

29a. Twigs, and sometimes undersides of younger leaves, densely covered with rusty brown or silvery speckles or scales (these are visible to the naked eye). The scales may grow so closely together on the leaves that they overlap, giving the undersides a distinctly metallic silvery sheen. Buds may be flanked by budlike stipules. Leaf elliptical and smooth-edged (although it may sometimes appear wavy). A small tree or tall shrub, often of old fields and waste places, that sometimes grows in dense stands or clumps.

Elaeagnus spp., including *E. umbellata*, autumn olive, which has thorns, though they may be rare and scattered, and *E. commutata*, American olive or silverberry, which lacks thorns.

29b. Neither rusty brown and silvery speckles nor scales are present on twigs and leaves, although the leaf undersides may have brown speckles and scales; undersides of leaves do not have metallic, silvery sheen. Go to 30.

30a. Undersides of leaves densely covered with brown scales, but silvery scales absent; upper surface of leaves may have scattered silvery scales; leaves small (usually less than 1 inch long), and may appear very minutely toothed or smooth-edged. A long spray or cluster of stalked flower buds or perhaps capsules may also be present at the ends of the twigs, each bud or capsule separated by a very small leaf on this cluster (Fig. 56). A small shrub, usually under 2 feet tall, growing in dense patches along water or in open, boggy areas. *Chamaedaphne calyculata*, leatherleaf.

30b. Undersides of leaves are not covered with rusty brown speckles; does not have the combination of features described above. Go to 31.

31a. Tiny, dark triangular stipules or stipule scars flank the leaf stems or leaf scars (use hand lens and compare to Figs. 26, 31, and 33). The stipules and stipule scars are very dark—almost black, but are easy to miss because they are so small. One bundle scar; buds have two or four paired bud scales. *Ilex spp.*, hollies and inkberry. See chapter 6.

31b. Tiny, dark stipules or stipule scars as described above are not present. Some plants have longer stipules that may resemble those described above, particularly late in the growing season. In that case, the plant has three bundle scars. Go to 32.

32a. Leaves with a toothed margin. Go to 40.

32b. Leaves with smooth edges, not toothed (one rare species listed below may have a few teeth restricted to the tips of some leaves. Go to 33.

33a. Pith solid but divided by woody partitions, which form faint lines in the pith, OR the pith is broken into solid and open areas (Fig. 50). Go to 34.

33b. Pith solid and homogeneous, not separated by woody partitions or broken into chambers. Go to 35.

34a. Solid, whitish pith is chambered by woody partitions; twigs and branches often form short spur branches that stand off from the main branches at an almost 90-degree angle (Fig. 50). Leaves on these spur branches are frequently clustered at the tips. Three bundle scars on leaf scars; true end buds; bark furrowed; base of leaf stems often reddish; small, dark fruit sometimes present. A common tree of wetter areas. *Nyssa sylvatica*, sour gum or black gum.

34b. Pith usually broken into open and solid areas; woody partitions, if present, separate open areas; twigs do not form short spur branches; one bundle scar forms a curved line; false end buds; bark broken up into small, square blocks; buds very dark, often with two scales; large, soft berrylike fruit, which turns orange when ripe in the fall. A tree found in various areas, but not common. *Diospyros virginiana*, persimmon.

35a. Leaves somewhat thickened and leathery (or waxy), and persisting over winter; leaves may appear clustered at the ends of the twigs, making the growth pattern seem whorled; twigs and leaf stems green and reddish. A tall, gnarly bush with twisted branches. *Kalmia latifolia*, mountain laurel (Fig. 19).

35b. Leaves thin, not leathery or waxy. Go to 36.

36a. Crushed leaves and twigs have a pleasant, spicy smell; three bundle scars; false end buds; buds with two or three bud scales. *Lindera benzoin*, spicebush.

36b. Crushed leaves and twigs have no spicy odor. Go to 37.

37a. Buds long, pointed; true end buds; leaves have a bristle tip (and some may have teeth near the end); dull reddish or yellowish fruits may be present in late summer. Rare populations restricted to western edge of the Pine Barrens. *Nemopanthus mucronatus*, catberry or mountain holly.

37b. Buds small, false end buds. Go to 38.

38a. Trees with very dark, almost blackish buds, often with two scales; pith usually broken into open and solid areas; fruit soft, large, and berrylike, turning orange when ripe in the fall; a tree with distinctive bark that is broken up into small, square, raised blocks about 1–2 inches square. This small tree is found in various areas, although it is not common.
Diospyros virginiana, persimmon.

38b. Shrubs; buds not blackish, typically reddish and with four or more visible scales; pith solid; fruit a cluster of capsules that may perist. *Lyonia spp.*
Go to 39.

39a. Small, round, reddish buds; woody, urn-shaped capsules may be present in clusters. *Lyonia mariana,* staggerbush (Figs. 48 and 57).

39b. Similar to the above, but leaves may be fine-toothed; woody capsules are nearly round, and buds have only two visible scales.
Lyonia ligustrina, maleberry (Fig. 46).

40. All of the following plants have leaves with a toothed margin.

40a. Broken bark of twigs has an unpleasant "bitter almond" odor (to smell what is a naturally occurring form of cyanide, scrape the bark with your thumbnail to roughen it); two small swellings, or "glands," usually flank the upper part of the leaf stem or the lower portion of the leaf blade (these may look like the lowest teeth of the leaf edges); bark of twigs, branches, and younger portion of tree or shrub smooth, brown with lighter cross bands; buds have more than three scales; three bundle scars. Most are thornless, but a few species have thorns.
Prunus spp., cherries and plums (Figs. 6, 22, and 58. See chapter 6.)

40b. Broken bark does not have the pungent, rank odor of bitter almonds; no swellings flanking the leaf stem or blade. Go to 41.

41a. Lowest bud scale of the lateral buds situated directly above, and centered over, the leaf stem or scar (Fig. 38); leaf stem long and often flattened (this makes the leaf tremble in the wind); leaf has three to five main veins, which meet where the leaf stem joins the leaf; young bark smooth and greenish. *Populus spp.*, poplars and aspens. See chapter 6.

41b. Lowest bud scale not situated directly above the leaf scar; placed either to one side or paired and flanking the center of the leaf scar; leaf stem round. Go to 42.

42a. Lateral and end buds attach to twig with a short stalk that may be obscured by a large stipule (which later drops off); buds covered by a single scale. Leaf elliptical; may be double-toothed or single-toothed and wavy-edged; leaf scars triangular; pith triangular. The fruit is a small, hard "cone" that stands erect; flowers a drooping cluster, looking like what is seen in the birches. *Alnus serrulata*, common or smooth alder.

42b. Buds, except flower buds, not stalked (if they appear so, then with many scales); leaves and fruit various, but the latter not conelike; pith round. Plants with short spur branches may appear to have stalked flower buds, but spur branches will typically have leaf scars on them. Go to 43.

43a. Leaf with single teeth. Go to 45.

43b. Leaf with double teeth. Go to 44.

44a. Leaf roughly triangular in shape (Fig. 28); bark is smooth with cross bands. In one species the bark comes off in scrolllike pieces. Bud scales lack dark tips; true end buds. A relatively common tree. *Betula spp.*, birches. See chapter 6.

44b. Leaf roughly oval in shape; bark dark and rough in older trees. Bud scales brown or reddish with distinctly darker tips. This is a species that is rare here, but most often found in wetter, settled areas in the northern portions of the Pine Barrens.
Ulmus americana, American elm (Fig. 29). Slippery elm, *Ulmus rubra,* may also be found.

45a. Upper surface of leaves' main vein has scattered dark glands, which resemble short, dark, thick hairs (Fig. 59). Narrow leaf scar has three bundle scars; buds are slender and reddish; bud scales have small notches at tip; fruit is a small, applelike berry; leaf base gradually tapers into leaf stem, forming a V.
Aronia spp., chokeberries. See chapter 6.

45b. Main vein's upper surface does not have whiskers, though other features may be present. Go to 46.

46a. Leaves with one main vein; base of leaf blade is symmetrical; leaves never lobed; bundle scars and end buds variable. Go to 50.

46b. Leaves with three main veins, which meet at or near asymmetrical base of leaf blade; three or more bundle scars; false end buds; some leaves may be irregularly lobed. Go to 47.

47a. Leaf tip usually long and tapering; three (sometimes more) bundle scars; pith usually chambered, especially adjacent to leaves or leaf scars; smooth bark becomes heavily warty over time. *Celtis occidentalis,* American hackberry.

47b. Leaf tip not long and tapering; pith not chambered; four or more bundle scars. Go to 48.

48a. Leaves longer than 5 inches and never lobed; buds with two to three scales. An introduced species that is very rare in the Pine Barrens. *Tilia americana,* American basswood.

48b. Leaves shorter than 4 inches, and some may be irregularly lobed; buds with more than three scales; berries present in the summer. *Morus spp.*, the mulberries (Fig. 9). Not native to the Pine Barrens. Go to 49.

49a. Upper surface of leaves has a coarse, gritty feel; the dark red or purple "berries" are sweet; milky sap. A tree or shrub with false end buds; buds have five to six scales. *Morus rubra,* red mulberry.

49b. Upper surface of leaves does not have a coarse, gritty feel; white berries not sweet; sap not milky. *Morus alba,* white mulberry.

50a. Leaves coarse-toothed; tips of teeth often form curls; leaf veins run to tips of teeth, forming bristle tips; false end buds. (Fig. 23). Go to 51.

50b. Leaves fine-toothed; leaf veins do not run to tips of teeth or form bristle tips. Go to 52.

51a. Leaves small (typically under 5 inches), undersides white-hairy. *Castanea pumila,* Eastern chinquapin.

51b. Leaves large (over 5 inches), undersides not white-hairy. A small tree or tall shrub that often sprouts from stumps. *Castanea dentata,* American chestnut.

52a. Leaves long and slender (at least seven times longer than wide); buds have a single scale, which covers the entire bud like a hood; twigs green and often soft. A tree or sapling often growing near water. *Salix nigra,* black willow (Fig. 36).

52b. Leaves not long and slender (length less than seven times width); bud scales do not cover the entire bud. Go to 53.

53a. Buds reddish or greenish, long, twisted, and pointed with dark-tipped scales; base of most leaves rounded and roughly forming a *U* or a very vague *V;* undersides of leaves not hairy, wooly, or whitish. *Amelanchier spp.,* serviceberries or Juneberries. See chapter 6.

53b. Buds not reddish or greenish with dark-tipped scales, not long and twisted; base of all leaves gradually tapers to leaf stem, forming a *V.* Go to 54.

54a. Twigs are typically short spurs with many rings, which are actually leaf scars; leaves may be clustered on these spurs; undersides of leaves hairy, wooly, or whitish; buds blunt and wooly; leaves may be coarsely toothed or may appear lobed in some cases; fruit a small, bitter apple. *Malus angustifolia,* Southern crabapple.

54b. Twigs are not short spurs with many rings; fruit not a small, bitter apple. Go to 55.

55a. True end buds. Go to 56.

55b. False end buds; leaves fine-toothed (sometimes not toothed in *Lyonia ligustrina*). Go to 57.

56a. Twigs tan or brown (only the youngest shoots are green); pith not chambered; one bundle scar. The thin bark of twigs flakes off in rectangular blocks or strips. Minute wooly hairs cover twigs. The two lowest bud scales of the end bud flank the bud and are as long or longer than the rest of the bud. These lowest bud scales are fleshy (Figs. 43 and 44). Long clusters of small, round woody capsules may be found. These do not open into halves (typically thirds or fifths). The capsules look like peppercorns but are fragile and easily crushed (Figs. 47 and 61). *Clethra alnifolia*, sweet pepperbush.

56b. Twigs green; pith faintly chambered; three bundle scars; several lateral buds typically line up above the leaves or leaf scars. End buds lack the two fleshy lower scales; these buds are about the same size as the lateral buds. Capsules may persist, but these are elongate and open into halves. An uncommon shrub of wet areas. *Itea virginica*, sweet spires.

57a. Very small, dark, rounded lateral buds with more than two bud scales; long spikes of green or reddish flower buds often persist for long periods of time; woody capsules, both open and closed, also may persist. *Leucothoe racemosa*, swamp sweetbells (Figs. 41, 45, and 59).

57b. Larger, slender lateral buds with only two bud scales; capsules on more open clusters and not forming reddish spikes. *Lyonia ligustrina*, maleberry (Fig. 46).

Chapter 6

Summer Keys to Selected Genera

Some species can be keyed out in the general keys outlined in chapter 5. Others can be identified using the following keys. Find the genus in one of the preceding keys and use the key for that genus.

Amelanchier spp., Juneberries or serviceberries

1a. Tall shrub or small tree growing to 20 feet, sometimes in a clump; young leaves sometimes slightly hairy beneath, mostly oblong, tips rounded or pointed. Go to 3.

1b. Small shrubs growing to 5 feet (usually less) and in patches, spreading from underground runners; leaves oval to almost round. Go to 2.

2a. Undersides of leaves hairy when mature (undersides of leaves of both this and the following species are white-wooly when young); leaves toothed almost to the base. *Amelanchier obovalis,* coastal serviceberry.

2b. Undersides of leaves not hairy when mature; the lower one-third of the leaves is not toothed. *Amelanchier stolonifera,* running serviceberry.

3a. Leaves sometimes have pointed tips and are slightly hairy beneath when young, sometimes staying hairy when old. *Amelanchier canadensis,* oblong-leaf serviceberry.

3b. Leaves most often have pointed tips and are densely hairy beneath when young, becoming hairless when old. *Amelanchier intermedia,* swamp serviceberry.

Aronia spp., chokeberries

1a. Undersides of leaves slightly or not at all hairy; twigs and buds slightly wooly, if at all.
Aronia melanocarpa, black chokeberry.

1b. Undersides of leaves have matted, wooly hair. Go to 2.

2a. Fruit red; mature twigs reddish; base of leaves rounded; undersides of leaves wooly.
Aronia arbutifolia, red chokeberry.

2b. Fruit purple; mature twigs brown; base of leaves tapers to the leaf stem; undersides of leaves densely wooly.
Aronia atropurpurea, purple chokeberry.

Betula spp., birches

1a. Bark shaggy, peeling off in thin rolls, and varying from reddish or greenish tan to brown; leaf triangular, without a long point; tree often has multiple trunks. *Betula nigra*, river birch.

1b. Bark whitish, not peeling as above, and not shaggy; leaf long-pointed. Go to 2.

2a. Leaves have a long tapering tip; undersides light green; twigs reddish and warty; buds not gummy; trunks commonly have dark chevrons (sergeant's stripes) at base of branches.
Betula populifolia, gray birch (Figs. 26 and 27).

2b. Leaves long-pointed but not so long as the previous, shiny above and beneath; twigs densely hairy; buds gummy; chevrons fewer or absent. *Betula alba*, European white birch.

Carya spp., hickories

1a. End buds under 3/8 inch; twigs slender; twigs and undersides of leaves not hairy when mature. Go to 3.

1b. End buds over 1/2 inch; twigs stout; twigs and undersides of leaves hairy when mature. Go to 2.

2a. Relatively common in the Pine Barrens; bark of older trees furrowed, forming a tight network that adheres to the tree; leaves have seven to nine leaflets. *Carya tomentosa,* mockernut hickory.

2b. Rare in the Pine Barrens; bark of older trees shaggy, portions detaching from the tree; leaves typically have five but sometimes seven leaflets. *Carya ovata,* shagbark hickory.

3a. End buds are yellow (sometimes yellow-orange), slender, and with paired scales; found mostly along the western edge of the Pine Barrens on richer soils. *Carya cordiformis,* bitternut hickory.

3b. End buds not yellow; scales overlap, not paired. Go to 4.

4a. Bark scaly or shaggy in older trees; stems of leaves and leaflets sometimes reddish; undersides of leaves have small, yellowish scales. Rare in the Pine Barrens. *Carya ovalis,* red hickory.

4b. Bark of older trees furrowed; undersides of leaves do not have small, yellowish scales. Go to 5.

5a. Midribs of leaves and leaflets are hairy underneath; leaves have seven to nine leaflets. Rare in the Pine Barrens. *Carya pallida,* sand hickory.

5b. Leaves and midribs hairless when mature; leaves typically have five (sometimes seven) leaflets. Common in the Pine Barrens. *Carya glabra,* pignut hickory.

Gaylussacia spp., huckleberries

1a. Shrubs to 6 feet tall, often at least 3 feet tall; leaves dull green above and whitish beneath, with no resin dots on the upper surface; leaf buds have four to five scales. *Gaylussacia frondosa*, dangleberry or tall huckleberry.

1b. Shrubs typically less than 3 feet tall; leaves not whitened on undersides; resin dots sometimes found on upper surface of leaves; leaf buds have two to three scales, although flower buds are larger, with four to five scales. Go to 2.

- 2a. Upper surface of leaf has resin dots; height to 3 feet; leaf tapers gradually to a point; upper surface of older leaves not shiny; young shoots and leaves sticky. *Gaylussacia baccata*, black huckleberry.

- 2b. Upper surface of leaves may not have resin dots; height under 2 feet, typically less; leaf tip rounded with a small point, which is an extension of the main vein past the leaf margin; upper surface of older leaves shiny; young shoots and leaves not sticky. *Gaylussacia dumosa*, dwarf huckleberry.

Hypericum spp, St. Johnsworts and St. Peterswort

1a. Tall shrub, typically 4–6 feet; flowers white with five petals. *Hypericum densiflorum*, dense St. Johnswort.

1b. Small shrub, under 2 feet; flowers yellow with four petals. Go to 2.

- 2a. Mostly erect shrub under 2 feet (often smaller); leaves ½–1½ inches long; leaf base clasps the twig by partially surrounding it. *Hypericum crux-andreae*, St. Peterswort.

- 2b. Low shrub to 10 inches; leaves to ½ inch long, which taper slightly to the base and do not clasp the twig. *Hypericum hypericoides*, St. Andrew's cross.

Ilex spp., hollies, ink berries, and gall berries

1a. Leaf thin, not evergreen, and falling in autumn; margin of leaf is either toothed or has a wavy edge. Go to 3.

1b. Leaf leathery and evergreen, persisting on the plant over winter; leaves are either toothed only at the tip OR have a series of sharp prickles around the edge. Go to 2.

2a. Margin of leaf forms a series of sharp prickles or thorns; berries, if present, are red. *Ilex opaca*, American holly.

2b. Margin of leaf is smooth, except toward the end, where it forms a few teeth; berries, if present, are brown or blue-black; twigs and branches green. *Ilex glabra*, ink berry, or gallberry (Fig. 26).

3a. Leaves fine-toothed and hairless underneath; leaves elliptical, tapering to a point at the tip and also tapering to the leaf stem. *Ilex laevigata*, smooth winterberry holly (Figs. 31 and 33).

3b. Leaves more coarse-toothed and hairy underneath; hair may be limited to area along leaf veins; leaves more varied in shape, often more rounded. *Ilex verticillata*, winterberry holly.

Populus spp., poplars

1a. Leaf stem rounded in cross section; leaves with coarse teeth or small lobes, often hairy or wooly on the underside; bark grayish or whitish when young but darker near the base of the tree. *Populus alba*, white poplar.

1b. Leaf stem distinctly flattened, not rounded in cross section; older leaves lose hair on their undersides; bark grayish, often with a greenish tinge. Go to 2.

2a. Leaves coarse-toothed with up to fifteen pairs of teeth; buds gray and hairy.
Populus grandidentata, big-toothed aspen (Fig. 38).

2b. Leaves finely toothed with over twenty pairs of teeth, often ending in a tapering tip; buds brown and glossy.
Populus tremuloides, trembling or quaking aspen.

Prunus spp., cherries and plums

1a. Some branches modified into thorns; older leaves hairless underneath; younger leaves may be hairy. Leaf stem may lack a pair of small swellings where the leaf blade joins the stem. Toothed leaves may have double teeth.
Prunus americana, American plum.

1b. Branches not modified into thorns; leaf undersides have hair, at least along the main vein. Go to 2.

2a. Main vein on underside of leaf is flanked with brown or white hairs; true end bud; a tree or sapling; twig and end bud mostly hairless. *Prunus serotina*, wild black cherry (Figs. 22 and 58).

2b. Leaf undersides have fine hairs, which are not limited to the area flanking the main vein; false end bud; twig and end bud hairy; a low-branched shrub. *Prunus maritima*, beach plum.

Quercus spp., the oaks

Leaves of the oaks are variable. Those exposed to more light and on the upper branches of the tree have deeper and more pronounced lobing than those in shade on the lower branches.

1a. Leaves elliptical and lacking either teeth or lobes; the base of the narrow leaves tapers to the leaf stem, and the tip tapers to a point. This leaf does not look at all like a typical oak leaf but is more "willowlike."
Quercus phellos, willow oak (Fig. 62).

1b. Leaves not elliptical and narrow but have either lobes or teeth, or are broader with several bristle tips. Go to 2.

2a. Leaves with lobes that end in bristle tips; leaves may have lobes or teeth, each of which ends with a bristle tip, or leaves may be broad without apparent lobes. In either case, look for bristle tips, which are extensions of the veins.
Go to 8.

2b. Leaves have no bristle tips; veins do not extend past the leaf edge; leaves lobed or have coarse teeth. Go to 3.

3a. Leaves not deeply lobed, but have either a series of large, rounded teeth or small lobes, which extend less than a quarter of the distance from the edge of the leaf to the midvein (Fig. 63). Go to 5.

3b. Leaves deeply lobed with the cuts between the lobes extending from the edge of the leaf at least halfway to the midvein (Figs. 14 and 15, for example). Go to 4.

4a. Leaves leathery, hairy underneath, with the three large lobes often forming a distinctive cross shape; there may be small lower lobes near the base that often angle upwards, looking somewhat like an arrowhead pointing down; twigs and end buds hairy; bark brownish. *Quercus stellata,* post oak (Fig. 64).

4b. Leaves not leathery and generally hairless underneath; leaves more regularly lobed, with a series of more or less equal-sized lobes (you will not see three large lobes forming a cross). End buds and twigs hairless; bark light grayish and forming thin, rectangular scales. The common oak tree with light-colored bark that is found in the Pine Barrens. *Quercus alba,* white oak (Fig. 14).

5a. Leaves have irregular teeth or shallow lobes, typically fewer than six pairs; acorns are stalked; end buds are chestnut brown; bark is grayish, flaky, and resembles that of white oak. A rare oak tree of wetlands. *Quercus bicolor,* swamp white or swamp oak.

5b. Leaves have regular, rounded teeth or a regular wavy edge. Go to 6.

6a. Shrubs; leaves small, generally under 4 inches, with fewer than eight pairs of shallow teeth (or waves); end bud small (under 3⁄16 inch) and not sharp. *Quercus prinoides,* dwarf or dwarf chestnut oak (Fig. 63).

6b. Trees; leaves longer than 5 inches, with eight or more pairs of rounded teeth (or wavy-edged with eight or more pairs of waves); end bud large (over 3⁄16 inch) and sharp. Go to 7.

7a. Trees with distinctive, deeply furrowed, bark; fissures in the bark can be over 1 inch deep; leaves slightly hairy underneath. *Quercus prinus,* chestnut oak.

7b. Bark not deeply furrowed but scaly; leaves more hairy underneath. *Quercus michauxii,* basket oak.

8a. Growth form is a tree, usually with a straight trunk. Go to 10.

8b. Growth form is a shrub that is typically not straight but more branched near the ground and scrubby. Go to 9.

9a. Leaves weakly lobed or not lobed, much wider toward tip and narrowing toward leaf stem; the leathery leaves are sometimes shaped like a rounded triangle with the apex attached to the leaf stem. Twigs wooly; buds wooly, angled, sharp, and almost 1⁄4 inch long. *Quercus marilandica,* blackjack oak.

9b. Leaves usually have more than five lobes, often with those near the base or middle portion of the leaf more prominent. Twigs hairless; buds relatively hairless, straight, dull, and closer to ⅛ inch long.
Quercus ilicifolia, scrub or bear oak (Fig. 65).

10a. Leaves very deeply lobed with five lobes; the three end lobes are long and slender while those at the base of the leaf are smaller. Leaves near the top of the tree look like bird's feet because of the three slender and prominent lobes toward the end of the leaf; end buds hairy; a tree or straight shrub.
Quercus falcata, Spanish or Southern red oak (Fig. 66).

10b. Leaves with more than five lobes, these more even-sized, the terminal lobes not long and slender and not resembling bird's feet. Go to 11.

11. The following two oaks often hybridize in the Pine Barrens, making it difficult to identify some individuals accurately as scarlet or black oak.

11a. Leaves deeply lobed; end buds almost ¼ inch long, usually blunt, and slightly hairy; older bark grooved. This is the common oak tree with bristle-tipped leaves in the Pine Barrens. *Quercus coccinea*, scarlet oak (Fig. 15).

11b. Leaves typically not deeply but moderately lobed; end buds ¼–½ inch long, pointed and usually sharp, densely grayish-hairy, and set at an angle to the line of the twig; older bark dark and blocky, inner bark orange.
Quercus velutina, black oak.

Rosa spp., the roses

This is a varied and difficult group to key out. There are many cultivated varieties, and some have escaped or interbred with wild types. Botanists who specialize in this genus cannot agree on the number of species. I include four of the more common varieties.

1a. Seven to nine leaflets per compound leaf; stipules adhering to the base of the leaf stem have fringes or are comblike. *R. multiflora*, multiflora rose (Fig. 11).

1b. Most often seven or fewer leaflets; stipules adhering to the base of the leaf stem are not fringed. Go to 2.

2a. Height usually less than 3 feet and not much branched; many prickles along the stems between the leaf stalks; prickles variable in size but round in cross section and straight. *R. carolina*, Carolina, or prairie rose.

2b. Height usually 3–6 feet and stems branched; prickles curved. Go to 3.

3a. Leaves most often have seven leaflets, the edges finely toothed (about the width of a 0.5-mm pencil lead); stipules narrow, getting only slightly wider toward the end; prickles curved. *R. palustris*, swamp rose.

3b. Leaves have seven to nine leaflets, the edges more coarsely toothed (the length of each about twice the width of a 0.5-mm pencil lead); stipules widen toward the end; prickles slightly curved. *R. virginiana*, Virginia rose.

Rubus spp., blackberries and dewberries

This is another member of the rose family with many species that are difficult to identify, even for experts. The two main groups are the low-running dewberries and the upright blackberries, which may have arching canes. The latter are particularly confusing. The species listed below are the most common in the Pine Barrens.

1a. Growth form upright with canes mostly erect, sometimes arching over; the blackberries. Go to 3.

1b. Growth form mostly flattened and growing close to the ground; the dewberries. Go to 2.

2a. Scattered, stout prickles; leaves dull, thin, light green, sometimes hairy, and with sharp teeth. *Rubus flagellaris*, prickly or Northern dewberry.

2b. Densely bristly (i.e., covered with stiff, hairlike bristles rather than prickles); leaves shiny, slightly leathery, and with blunt teeth. *Rubus hispidus*, bristly dewberry.

3a. Very prickly, typically with pale, curved prickles that can be as long as ½ inch; leaves have leaflets with rounded or slightly pointed tips and single teeth; common. *Rubus cuneifolius*, sand blackberry.

3b. Scattered, stout, mostly straight prickles; the tips of the leaflets, especially the leaflet at the end of the leaf stem, are tapered; leaflets double-toothed. Go to 4.

Note: These last two species are particularly difficult to separate.

4a. Leaf stems prickly; mature canes purplish; terminal leaflet has a long, tapering tip. *Rubus allegheniensis*, Allegheny blackberry.

4b. Leaf stems hairy rather than prickly; terminal leaflet has a more pronounced tapering of the tip. *Rubus pensilvanicus,* Pennsylvania blackberry.

Smilax spp., greenbriers

1a. Leaves thick and leathery; vines climbing and rarely forming dense tangles; a greenbrier of wetlands. *Smilax laurifolia,* laurel greenbrier.

1b. Leaves thin and not leathery; vines climbing and running on the ground, sometimes forming dense tangles. Go to 2.

2a. Berries red; prickles slender and scattered, limited to lower portions of plant. *Smilax walteri,* redberry greenbrier.

2b. Berries black; prickles throughout, including branches and twigs. Go to 3.

3a. Leaves vary from elliptical to heart-shaped; leaf undersides whitish, sometimes with patches of white on the upper surface. *Smilax glauca,* glaucous greenbrier.

3b. Leaves rounded, sometimes heart-shaped but without whitish color on leaf undersides. *Smilax rotundifolia,* round-leaf greenbrier.

Vaccinium spp., blueberries

1a. Plants typically short, under 2 feet and often under 1 foot; twigs never long and straight. Lowbush blueberries are typically found in dry woods. Go to 3.

1b. Plants typically tall shrubs (commonly 3–10 feet); twigs may be short but some can be longer than a foot and very straight. Highbush blueberries are typically found in wetlands or moist woods. Go to 2.

2a. Older leaves are hairless on the undersides, although there may be hair along the veins; leaves sometimes toothed; twigs slightly hairy or not; young branches green, sometimes also reddish. The common blueberry of wetlands. *Vaccinium corymbosum,* common highbush blueberry.

2b. Older leaves wooly or densely hairy on the undersides and never toothed; twigs very hairy; young branches green. A rare blueberry of wetlands. *Vaccinium atrococcum,* black highbush blueberry.

3a. Leaf edge has a few bristle-tipped teeth or a smooth margin; leaves whitish or pale on the undersides; leaf shape varies from egg-shaped to elliptical. The common lowbush blueberry of uplands. *Vaccinium vacillans,* early lowbush blueberry.

3b. Leaves have minute, bristle-tipped teeth and are bright green on undersides; leaf shape narrower than above; young branches sometimes grooved. A rare lowbush blueberry, which typically forms dense clumps. *Vaccinium angustifolium,* late lowbush blueberry.

Vitis spp., grapes

1a. Twigs green. Go to 4.

1b. Twigs and young leaf undersides red and hairy. Go to 2.

2a. Tendrils or fruit or flower clusters opposite almost every leaf. Go to 3.

2b. Some leaves do not have tendrils or fruit or flower clusters. More specifically, they are absent from every third leaf. *Vitis aestivalis*, summer grape.

3a. Leaf undersides red and hairy. *Vitis lambrusca*, fox grape.

3b. Leaf undersides of older leaves become whitish or hairless, although patches of hairs may remain. *V. novae-angliae*, New England grape.

4a. Leaves often deeply lobed; toothed margins with long, tapering tips, especially at the tip of the lobe; twigs round in cross section. *Vitis riparia*, riverbank grape.

4b. Leaves seldom lobed (rarely deeply lobed); long, tapering tips absent; twigs may be slightly angled. *Vitis vulpina*, frost grape.

Chapter 7

Winter Keys to Most Species

Use key A (chapter 5) for evergreen plants with needlelike, nail-like, or scalelike leaves because these plants remain largely unchanged over the course of the year. Use the keys below for broad-leaf plants, both those that retain their leaves and those that lose their leaves over winter.

E. Broad-Leaf Plants That Retain Green Leaves over Winter

1a. Thorny vine; leaves thick and leathery; tendrils present; vines climbing and rarely forming dense tangles. A greenbrier of wetlands. *Smilax laurifolia*, laurel greenbrier.

1b. Not a thorny vine. Go to 2.

2a. Upright tree or shrub, typically taller than 6 inches. Go to 10.

2b. Low creeping shrub or a creeping or climbing vine. Go to 3.

3a. Leaves and leaf scars opposite. Go to 4.

3b. Leaves and leaf scars alternate. Go to 5.

4a. Leaves, twigs, and stems very hairy; entire leaf margin usually smooth but with a hairy fringe; leaves usually elliptical in shape with a tapering base and much larger than 1 inch. This invasive plant often forms dense tangles or climbs on other plants and structures, frequently in disturbed areas. *Lonicera japonica*, Japanese honeysuckle.

4b. Leaves, twigs, and stems not hairy; leaf margin smooth or with slight undulations; leaf shape varies from heart-shaped to oval; leaves small (under 1 inch) with a rounded base (i.e., not tapering). A small, green, barely woody, trailing shrub of wetlands. *Mitchella repens*, partridgeberry.

5a. Plants low (usually less than 6 inches), solitary or forming small groups but not dense mats; plants slightly herbaceous and joined by underground stems. Go to 6.

5b. Plants forming dense mats on the surface of the ground. Go to 8.

6a. Crushed leaves have a pleasant, spicy scent (teaberry or wintergreen); leaves nearly round, with no teeth. *Gaultheria procumbens*, wintergreen or teaberry.

6b. Leaves do not have the pleasant, spicy smell described above; leaves fleshy and leathery with few, coarse teeth. Go to 7.

7a. Leaves have a distinctive whitish streak down the center. *Chimaphila maculata*, spotted wintergreen (Fig. 24).

7b. Leaves do not have a whitish streak. *Chimaphila umbellata*, princess pine.

8a. Leaves large (1–3 inches long), hairy underneath and sometimes above; leaves almost round with a long, usually hairy leaf stem. *Epigaea repens*, trailing arbutus or mayflower.

8b. Leaves smaller, about 1 inch long, and oval or spatula-shaped. Go to 9.

9a. A plant of wetlands and wet depressions; twigs hairless; leaves slightly whitened underneath and averaging about ½ inch in length; widest point of leaf about halfway from base to tip; soft, sour red berries may be present. *Vaccinium macrocarpon*, cranberry.

9b. A plant of dry uplands; twigs typically hairy; bark shreddy; leaves not slightly whitened underneath; leaves average about 1 inch in length with widest point closer to base. Fruit a small, dry berry. *Arctostaphylos uva-ursi*, evergreen bearberry.

10a. Trees, saplings, or shrubs with alternate leaves and leaf scars. Go to 12.

10b. Trees, saplings, or shrubs with opposite leaves and leaf scars. Go to 11.

11a. Leaves large (1–2 inches long), sometimes in whorls of three; leaves thin, light green. A common small shrub of pine woods. *Kalmia angustifolia,* sheep laurel or sheepkill.

11b. Leaves small (less than ½ inch), sometimes alternate. Leaves thick, leathery. A rare plant of sandy areas. *Leiophyllum buxifolium,* sand myrtle.

12a. Barely woody shrub with graceful, curving branches and very small leaves; leaves may be single and elliptical or compound with leaflets in threes; twigs green, very thin, and markedly grooved; the end of the twig is typically lost over winter; buds and leaf scars minute. *Cytisus scoparius,* Scotch broom.

12b. Woody shrub or tree without the cluster of features described above. Go to 13.

13a. Resin dots present on lower surface of leaves and sometimes on upper surface, stems, and buds. (Use a hand lens to see resin dots, which are small, yellow globules that catch and reflect light like tiny droplets of pitch or resin.) Crushed leaves have pleasant, spicy odor; leaves smooth-edged, although a few teeth may be present toward the tip; small, hard, waxy, light-colored berries may grow in clusters near the leaf bases. *Myrica cerifera,* waxmyrtle.

13b. Resin dots and other features described above are absent. Go to 14.

14a. Undersides of leaves covered with dense, brown scales; leaves small (usually less than 1 inch) and appear very minutely toothed or may be smooth-edged; a long cluster of flower buds (or perhaps capsules) may

be present at the ends of the twigs (each bud or capsule in this cluster is separated by a very small leaf); a small shrub (under 2 feet), typically growing in dense patches along water or in open, boggy areas.
Chamaedaphne calyculata, leatherleaf.

14b. Undersides of leaves not covered with dense, brown scales; leaves larger or, if small, then with a few teeth only at the end. Go to 15.

15a. Leaves smaller than 3 inches long; leaves have either a few teeth at the end or a few sharp spines along the edge; tiny paired triangular stipules, or stipule scars, flank the leaf stems or leaf scars. (Use hand lens.) Stipules and stipule scars are very dark, almost black. Two or four paired bud scales; one bundle scar. *Ilex spp.*, hollies and inkberry (Fig. 26). Go to 18.

15b. Leaves larger than 3 inches long and with a smooth edge; tiny stipules or stipule scars as described above are absent. Go to 16.

16a. Stipule scar forms a line or ring around the twig where the leaf stem attaches to the twig; crushed leaf has a pleasant, spicy smell; leaf scar has many bundle scars; large end bud is covered by a single scale; a few leaves with silvery or whitish undersides limited to the top of the tree. A thin tree or sapling of wet areas. *Magnolia virginiana*, sweetbay magnolia (Fig. 17).

16b. Ringlike stipule scar absent from twigs; crushed leaves have no spicy smell; undersides of leaves not whitish; buds have more than one scale; many leaves. An often tall, gnarly shrub. Go to 17.

17a. Common plant throughout the Pine Barrens; end buds are small; rusty-colored, hairy capsules may be present. *Kalmia latifolia*, mountain laurel (Fig. 19).

17b. Rare shrub limited to a few populations along the western border of the Pine Barrens; end buds large, many times larger than lateral buds, and with many bud scales; leaves typically to 8 or more inches long with hairy undersides and a slightly rolled edge; twigs hairy; capsules not rusty-colored. *Rhododendron maximum*, great laurel.

18a. The margin of the leaf forms a series of sharp prickles or thorns; berries, if present, are red. *Ilex opaca*, American holly.

18b. The margin of the leaf is smooth except toward the end, where it forms a few teeth; berries, if present, are brown or blue-black; twigs and branches green. *Ilex glabra*, ink berry, or gallberry (Fig. 26).

F. Leafless Plants with Opposite Leaf Scars

Use this key for plants that lose their leaves over winter and have opposite leaf scars. In the following key, reference is sometimes made to figures that illustrate points in the text. Because most of these drawings were done during the growing season, they show the plants with leaves that are very likely not present over winter. Take this present into consideration when comparing your specimen to the illustration.

1a. One bundle scar, sometimes forming a straight or curved line. Go to 2.

1b. Three or more bundle scars. Go to 5.

2a. Leaf scars sometimes in whorls of three or even four; bundle scar forms a curved line resembling the letter *U;* side buds not evident, submerged in the bark; false end buds; a hard, ball-like fruit about 1 inch in diameter may be present. A tall shrub almost always found near water. *Cephalanthus occidentalis*, buttonbush.

2b. Leaf scars never in whorls of three or more; lateral buds evident, although they may be small; true end buds. Go to 3.

3a. Leaf scars connected by a line; bundle scar forms a single dot; small lateral buds have two scales. A small shrub.
Hypericum densiflorum, dense St. Johnswort; *H. crux-andreae*, St. Peterswort; and *H. hypericoides*, St. Andrew's cross. These species are difficult to separate in the winter.

3b. Leaf scars not connected by a line; bundle scar forms a line; lateral buds with four or more bud scales. Go to 4.

4a. Lateral buds with four or fewer bud scales; leaf scar not raised; twigs thicker than $1/16$ inches in diameter. A rare plant restricted to areas near water courses in the southern portion of the Pine Barrens. *Chionanthus virginicus*, fringe tree.

4b. Lateral buds usually with more than four bud scales evident; leaf scar raised; twigs thin, usually $1/16$ inch or smaller in diameter. An introduced plant common in waste places.
Ligustrum vulgare, common privet.

5a. Three bundle scars. Go to 6.

5b. More than three bundle scars. Be careful to examine several leaf scars to determine whether there are three, or more than three, bundle scars. Go to 11.

6a. Pith of older branches is hollow; old bud scales persist at the base of the twigs where these arise from the previous year's growth. A shrub with slender branches and small, rounded buds that typically have three scales.
Lonicera tatarica, Tartarian honeysuckle.

6b. Pith solid; scales of old buds do not remain to separate the twigs from the branches. Go to 7.

7a. A few of the end buds are actually flower buds. These are round and distinctively stalked. The other end buds resemble lateral buds. (See Fig. 40 for an illustration of this bud.) Twigs distinctively colored green to purple; lateral buds have two scales, which meet in the center like the halves of a clam shell (Japanese maple has a similar bud, but these trees lack the stalked bud and the greenish-purplish twigs).
Cornus florida, flowering dogwood.

7b. End buds not expanded and stalked; twigs variously colored but not both green and purple; lateral buds not as described above. Go to 8.

8a. A tree or shrublike sapling with smooth, gray bark; buds red, with four or more scales; buds may cluster at the leaf scars or at the ends of twigs; twigs reddish or reddish brown; some branches form short spurs with many leaf scars clustered closely together.
Acer rubrum, red or swamp maple, the common maple of wet areas in southern New Jersey.

8b. Bark, buds, and scales not as above. Go to 9.

9a. Buds typically long, at least three times longer than wide, often lying pressed flat against the branch and sometimes slightly curved; short, spurlike branches are not present. Shrubs often have many stems; twigs long and very slender, sometimes faintly ridged (almost six-sided).
Viburnum spp., the arrowwoods. See chapter 8.

9b. Buds shorter than above and sometimes rounded slightly, not lying right against the branch and not curved; twigs slender, although short, spurlike branches with many leaf scars may also be present. Trees typically have one trunk (although saplings and small trees may have several trunks). *Acer spp.*, the maples. Go to 10.

10a. End buds paired; leaf scar markedly raised; base of lateral bud hairy where it joins the leaf scar; sap clear. This small, gnarly tree is an escaped ornamental. *Acer palmatum*, Japanese maple.

10b. End buds not paired, leaf scar not markedly raised, base of lateral bud not hairy as described above; sap milky. Another introduced species. *Acer platanoides*, Norway maple.

11. More than three bundle scars.

11a. True end buds; leaf scars and buds may be crowded toward the tip of the twigs, making the tip look like it has clustered end buds. A tree or sapling with greenish twigs. *Fraxinus pennsylvanica*, green ash.

11b. Single true end bud; lacking the above combination of characteristics. Go to 12.

12a. Leaf scars connected by a line; bundle scars arranged in a U-shaped line. Pith thick and white, twigs only slightly woody and with raised (or warty) lenticles. A shrub. *Sambucus canadensis*, common elderberry.

12b. Leaf scars not connected by a line; bundle scars arranged in a circle. Pith may be white, but the twigs and branches are very woody. A tree. Go to 13.

13a. Pith either chambered or hollow; leaf scars paired or in whorls of more than two; fruit woody and rounded. *Paulownia tomentosa*, princess tree.

13b. Pith solid and whitish; leaf scars paired and never in whorls; fruit woody and long. *Catalpa speciosa*, catalpa or catawba.

G. Leafless Plants Having Alternate Leaf Scars

Use this key for plants that lose their leaves over winter and have alternate leaf scars. As in the previous key, illustrations often show the plants with leaves because the drawings were done during the growing season. Keep this in mind when comparing your specimen, which will probably not have leaves, to the illustrations, which will show them.

1a. Thorns or spines present. Go to 2.

1b. Thorns or spines absent. Go to 9.

2a. An upright tree or shrub; twigs and branches mostly brown. Go to 5.

2b. A climbing vine or arching, vinelike shrub; twigs and branches green. Go to 3.

3a. A climbing vine with tendrils; often forms dense clumps or tangles; dark blue, black, or sometimes red berries can be present. *Smilax spp.*, the greenbriers. See chapter 8.

3b. A sprawling, arching, or sometimes climbing vine without tendrils. Go to 4.

4a. Leaf stems mostly lost in winter, revealing a very narrow leaf scar that wraps about halfway around the stem; three bundle scars, one in the middle of the leaf scar and the other two at the ends. *Rosa spp.*, the roses. See chapter 8.

4b. Leaf stems remain over winter; leaf scars and bundle scars not evident. *Rubus spp.*, the blackberries and dewberries. See chapter 8.

5. Upright trees and shrubs with thorns or spines.

5a. Twigs densely covered with rusty brown or silvery scales that are visible to the naked eye; buds may be flanked by budlike stipules; spines are modified branches, often confined to the lower portion of the plant. A small tree or tall shrub often found in old fields and waste places and sometimes growing in dense stands or clumps.
Elaeagnus umbellata, autumn olive.

5b. Twigs not as above; no rusty brown or silvery scales. Go to 6.

6a. True end buds. Go to 8.

6b. False end buds. Go to 7.

7a. Leaf scars narrow; scattered thorns may be present; these are long modified branches that end in a sharp point, and they may have buds and leaf scars on them; thorns are neither paired nor adjacent to the leaf scars. Broken bark of twigs has an unpleasant "bitter almond" smell; to release this odor, which is cyanide, scrape the bark with your nail; bark of twigs, branches, and younger portion of tree or shrub smooth, brown, with lighter cross bands; buds have more than three scales; three bundle scars.
Prunus americana, American plum.

7b. Leaf scars rounded; two thorns flanking each leaf scar; these thorns are short and are not modified branches and therefore, they lack leaf scars or buds; lateral buds may be hidden in the leaf scars; no bitter almond smell of cyanide. *Robinia spp.*, the locusts. See chapter 8.

8a. Few thorns; thorns are modified branches with leaf scars and sometimes buds, or there may be short, spurlike branches that often have many closely spaced growth rings encircling them.
Malus angustifolia, Southern crabapple.

8b. Many thorns which lack leaf scars and buds. *Crataegus uniflora,* dwarf hawthorn.

9. None of the following plants have thorns.

9a. Upright trees or shrubs. Go to 14.

9b. Low, creeping shrubs or woody vines. Go to 10.

10a. A running or climbing vine, sometimes slightly upright, which may grow as a shrub in some locales; stems hairy brown with aerial rootlets, the long hairs attaching to the surface of trees or other objects; clusters of white berries may be present. *Toxicodendron radicans,* poison ivy, a toxic plant (Fig. 1).

10b. Stems not densely hairy or, if hairy, then only slightly so; no aerial rootlets. Go to 11.

Note: Do not confuse aerial rootlets with occasional tendrils that may be present in some of the following species. Aerial rootlets, such as those seen in poison ivy, are brown and typically give the plant a very wooly appearance. If they are present, they can easily be seen from at least an arm's length away. Tendrils (see Fig. 32 for an example) most often arise at the base of a leaf or at the leaf node.

11a. Upright trees or shrubs without thorns. Go to 14.

11b. Not a low, creeping shrub; a climbing or sprawling vine. Go to 12.

12a. Vines that climb without tendrils; buds long and covered with soft hairs; one bundle scar, which forms a line; often a large vine with twisted bark. *Wisteria frutescens,* wisteria.

12b. Vines that climb using tendrils. Go to 13.

13a. Pith brownish, with woody partitions opposite the leaf scars; frequently a climbing vine that most often grows upwards, has a large-diameter stem, and brown, shreddy bark.
Vitis spp., the grapes. See chapter 8.

13b. Whitish pith that is continuous, i.e., lacking woody partitions; a sprawling and sometimes climbing vine not having a large-diameter stem and not having brown, shreddy bark.
Parthenocissus quinquefolia, Virginia creeper.

14a. Stems very thin, green, and ridged or furrowed, and angular in cross section; leaf scars small and round; buds very small; leaves may persist and are very small and either elliptical or, the lower ones especially, compound with three leaflets. A small, arching shrub with barely woody stems, the tip often being lost over winter. *Cytisus scoparius*, Scotch broom.

14b. Stems brown, reddish, or green (if green, then not a small, arching shrub with grooved or furrowed stems as described above). Go to 15.

15a. Bundle scars form three U- or C-shaped lines, each of which is actually made up of several bundle scars; leaf scars large and often with three lobes; twigs thick, the pith chambered, being usually broken up into open and closed areas; buds white and wooly. A tree with true end buds. *Juglans nigra*, black walnut (Fig. 49).

15b. Bundle scars do not form U-shaped lines; one, three, or more than three bundle scars. Go to 16.

16a. Three or more bundle scars. Go to 30.

16b. One bundle scar, or bundle scars indistinct. Go to 17.

17a. Clustered end buds; the central one is a flower bud and much larger than the others around it; these surrounding buds may often be tiny in comparison. Growth sometimes compressed, the branches and leaf scars sometimes appearing whorled. *Rhododendron spp.* (Fig. 35).

There are two common species of *Rhododendron* throughout the Pine Barrens. The swamp azalea (*Rhododendron viscosum*) has hairy twigs and very hairy buds. The pink azalea (*Rhododendron periclymenoides*) is less hairy.

17b. Single end bud or no end bud. Go to 18.

18a. Twigs densely covered with rusty brown or silvery scales that are visible to the naked eye; buds may be flanked by budlike stipules. A small tree or tall shrub, often of old fields and waste places, and growing in dense stands or clumps. *Elaeagnus commutata*, silverberry.

18b. Twigs not as above; do not have rusty brown or silvery scales. Go to 19.

19a. Twigs and young branches green, sometimes with red along one side, but always speckled with many, very tiny white dots (use a hand lens and compare twigs to those seen in Fig. 37). *Vaccinium spp.*, the blueberries. See chapter 8.

19b. Twigs not speckled with numerous, tiny white dots, although larger resin dots, scattered lenticels, or darker spots may be present. Go to 20.

20a. Buds and twigs may have scattered resin dots (use hand lens). This feature is hard to see because the resin dots are few and scattered. However, this is a distinctive feature of only a few plants. Go to 21.

20b. Young buds and twigs do not have resin dots. Go to 23.

21a. Crushed buds and young twigs have a pleasant, spicy smell; buds small and only of one size; three bundle scars, although the two lateral ones are often difficult to see. Fruit not a black berry. Go to 22.

21b. Crushed buds and twigs do not have a spicy smell; one bundle scar; buds of two sizes, larger flower buds and the smaller lateral and terminal buds; fruit a berry that is not typically found over winter. When it is, the blackberry is shriveled up and dried out. *Gaylussacia spp.*, the huckleberries. See chapter 8.

22a. Twigs and buds with abundant resin dots; twigs mostly hairless; growth compressed toward the tip of the twig, making the buds near the tip seem whorled or clustered; dried leaves may persist; these are elliptical and bear a few teeth only at the tip. A shrub that sometimes grows quite large, often in clumps. *Myrica pensylvanica,* bayberry.

22b. Twigs and buds with few resin dots; a small shrub with thin, very hairy twigs; dead leaves long, very thin, and either coarsely toothed or lobed, often persisting until late winter; branches and leaves have a fernlike appearance. *Comptonia peregrina,* sweet fern (Fig. 25).

23a. Twigs either with false terminal buds or each with a cluster of flower buds. Go to 27.

23b. Twigs with true end buds. Note: Do not confuse flower buds, which may be arranged in a thin spray in some of these species, with true end buds. Go to 24.

24a. Broken twigs and roughened bark of twigs has a pleasant, spicy smell (although somewhat woody, with a minty-spicy taste); twigs and young branches green; bundle scars elongated; bud scales paired, usually three or more; buds large. *Sassafras albidum,* sassafras.

24b. Broken and crushed twigs do not have a spicy smell; lateral buds either have two bud scales or are very small and indistinct. Go to 25.

25a. The end buds are much larger than the lateral buds. The lowest bud scales of the end bud are somewhat fleshy and as long or longer than the rest of the bud (Fig. 44). Fruit is a spray or elongate cluster of delicate woody capsules, each one of which is easily broken (Fig. 47). This distinctive cluster often persists over winter. The thin bark of the twigs and young branches sometimes peels back in small squares. Twigs are covered by tiny tan hairs that may be hard to see even with a hand lens but which give the twig a fuzzy or dotted appearance. A very common tall shrub of wetlands or intermediate positions. *Clethra alnifolia,* sweet pepperbush.

25b. Tiny paired triangular stipules, or stipule scars, flank the leaf stems or leaf scars (use hand lens, Figs. 26, 31, and 33). Stipules and stipule scars are very dark—almost black; two or four paired bud scales; end buds and lateral buds much closer in size; fruit a bright orange-red berry that may persist. A less common shrub, often of very wet areas. *Ilex spp.,* the gallberry hollies.

Note: The hollies that lose their leaves over winter do not look at all like the holly trees you may recognize, although they are in the same genus. Go to 26.

26a. Buds with sharp pointed scales; twigs without hairs.
Ilex laevigata, smooth winterberry.

26b. Bud scales come to a point but more broadly; twigs may be either hairless or slightly fine-hairy. *Ilex verticillata*, winterberry.

27a. Pith usually broken into open and solid areas; woody partitions, if present, separate open areas; older bark distinctively broken up into small, rectangular blocks (each of which is 1–2 inches long and about an inch wide); buds very dark, often with two scales. A sapling or small tree found in various areas, but not common. *Diospyros virginiana*, persimmon.

27b. Buds not small or very dark; pith solid and not as described above; bark not square and blocky; a shrub. Go to 28.

28a. A long, reddish cluster of small flower buds often persists over winter; lateral buds are tiny and brown. Sometimes three generations of reproductive parts are present: the long cluster of flower buds, closed hard capsules bearing seeds, and open capsules from which seeds are shed (Figs. 41 and 45). The open capsules are more fragile than in the following species.
Leucothoe racemosa, swamp sweetbells or fetterbush.
Note: The name of the genus is pronounced lou-koh-thow'-ee.

28b. Long flower buds not present over winter; lateral buds larger and reddish; woody capsules often appear striped, the open capsules quite hard. *Lyonia spp.* Go to 29.

29a. Capsules are urn-shaped; lateral buds rounded, reddish, and with four or five scales; twigs brownish.

Lyonia mariana, staggerbush (Fig. 48). This is the more common species; it is named for the growth pattern, where the main branch zig-zags, or staggers, back and forth.

29b. Capsules rounded; lateral buds elongate and hugging the branch, with only two scales; twigs yellowish-greenish. *Lyonia ligustrina,* maleberry (Fig. 46).

30a. Three bundle scars. Go to 31.

30b. More than three bundle scars. Go to 47.

31a. Pointed buds, each entirely covered by one scale (Fig. 36); twigs light brown or yellowish brown, long and very thin; branches greenish; leaf scars thin, raised, and partially encircling the bud; leaf scars flanked by stipule scars or sometimes, black stipules; end buds false. A tree found near water.

Salix nigra, black willow.

31b. Buds not entirely covered by one scale. Go to 32.

32a. Twigs and buds have at least a few resin dots. Go to 33.

32b. Resin dots absent. Go to 34.

33a. Twigs and buds have abundant resin dots; twigs mostly hairless; growth compressed toward the tip of the twig, making the buds near the tip seem whorled or clustered; dried leaves may persist; these are elliptical and bear a few teeth only at the tip. A shrub that sometimes grows quite large, often in clumps. *Myrica pensylvanica,* bayberry.

33b. Twigs and buds have few resin dots; a small shrub with thin, very hairy twigs; dead leaves long, very thin, either coarsely toothed or lobed, and often persisting until late winter; branches and leaves have a fernlike appearance. *Comptonia peregrina*, sweet fern (Fig. 25).

34a. True end buds. Go to 39.

34b. False end buds or no end buds present on the plant. Go to 35.

35a. Crushed twigs and buds have a pronounced smell that is pleasant and spicy; stalked flower buds often flank the leaf scars and smaller lateral buds; lateral buds with paired bud scales. An uncommon, sometimes tall shrub of areas near the coast. *Lindera benzoin*, spicebush.

35b. Crushed twigs and buds have no spicy smell, or spicy smell faint; stalked flower buds not present; bud scales more than two. Go to 36.

36a. Twigs grey-green, thin, and distinctly furrowed (grooved) and angled. A tall shrub growing near the coast. *Baccharis halimifolia*, groundsel tree.

36b. A tall shrub or small tree without the characteristics listed above. Go to 37.

37a. Buds small and round; leaf scar lobed; pith round in cross section; bundle scars only three. *Albizzia julibrissin*, mimosa or albizzia.

37b. Buds larger and elongate; leaf scar not lobed, more elliptical instead; pith star-shaped in cross section, five-pointed; bundle scars sometimes more than three. Go to 38.

38a. Buds mostly downy or hairy. *Castanea pumila,* Eastern chinquapin.

38b. Buds mostly hairless. *Castanea dentata,* American chestnut.

39a. Buds stalked; woody, conelike fruits often persist over winter; these are on long, stiff stems. A shrub of wet areas. *Alnus serrulata,* common alder.

39b. Buds not stalked. Not a shrub but rather a sapling or tree. Of the species below, round woody fruits are found on *Liquidambar styraciflua,* but these have sharp points and are not conelike. Go to 40.

40a. Lowest bud scale of lateral buds directly above, and centered over, the leaf scar (Fig. 38); young bark smooth and greenish. *Populus spp.,* poplars and aspens. See chapter 8.

40b. Lowest bud scale of lateral buds not centered over the leaf scar but to one side. Go to 41.

41a. Pith solid but interrupted by woody partitions, or “diaphragms.” Go to 42.

41b. Pith solid, not interrupted by woody partitions. Go to 43.

42a. Twigs brown; woody capsules not present. A straight tree of wetlands whose long branches have many short spur or nail-like branches coming off at nearly right angles (Fig. 50). This pattern of branching is distinctive, making this common, wetland tree easy to identify from a distance. *Nyssa sylvatica,* black or sour gum.

42b. Twigs green; clusters of long woody capsules may be present over winter. A shrub without short spur branches as described above. *Itea virginica,* sweet spires.

43a. Large, hard, round fruit studded with sharp projections typically persists over winter; branches often have one or two long, corky fins (or ridges) running along the branch; crushed buds have a distinctive smell that some describe as spicy and pleasant, while others find the odor mildly distasteful or "soapy." *Liquidambar styraciflua,* sweet gum.

43b. Hard, round fruit described above is not present; crushed buds do not have a spicy smell, although some may have a sharp, unpleasant odor of bitter almonds. Go to 44.

44a. Crushed bark, twigs, and buds have a sharp, very unpleasant odor of bitter almonds (cyanide). *Prunus spp.,* cherries and plums. See chapter 8.

44b. Crushed parts do not have the unpleasant smell described above. Go to 45.

45a. Bark smooth and light, either white, gray, or reddish; the bark of young branches and twigs is often shiny reddish and marked by raised, horizontally elongate lenticles; buds hairless; lateral buds have only two to three scales. *Betula spp.,* the birches. See chapter 8.

45b. Bark does not have raised, horizontally elongate lenticles; buds hairy; lateral buds have more than three scales. Go to 46.

46. These last species of plants with three bundle scars are all in the rose family. Because of this, they share several features that may make them difficult to distinguish during the winter. This is particularly true for the last two genera.

46a. Buds twisted and pointed with dark-tipped scales; pith star-shaped in cross section; smooth gray bark on a trunk with longitudinal striations that make the smooth trunk seem ropey (or musclelike) in appearance.
Amelanchier spp., serviceberries or Juneberries. There are two groups of Juneberries, the smaller shrublike species and the taller saplinglike species. These are difficult to identify to species in the wintertime. See chapter 8 for the names of these.

46b. Buds notched at tip, not markedly darkened, not twisted as above; pith roughly round in cross section. *Aronia spp.*, chokeberries. See chapter 8.

47. Trees and shrubs with four or more bundle scars.

47a. End buds single or absent. Go to 49.

47b. End buds clustered, and they might be very small. Go to 48.

48a. Stipule scars present; buds tiny; bud scales few or not evident; end of twig expanded into three small ends. A rare escapee. *Hibiscus syriacus*, rose of Sharon.

48b. Stipule scars not present; buds larger, with many bud scales evident; end of twig enlarged but not expanded into three small ends. Common trees or gnarly shrubs.
Quercus spp., the oaks (Fig. 34). See chapter 8.

49a. Trees, saplings, or shrubs with false end buds. Go to 52.

49b. Trees or saplings, with true end buds. One shrub has true end buds that lack bud scales and are narrowed at the base (i.e., naked buds that are stalked). Go to 50.

50a. Shrubs with buds on short stalks; buds without scales; clusters of white berries often present over winter. This plant may also grow as a vine with long, brown aerial roots, giving the vine a hairy appearance. *Toxicodendron radicans*, poison ivy, a toxic plant (Fig. 1).

50b. Trees or saplings with buds that have two or more scales. Go to 51.

51a. A ringlike line (or stipule scar) encircles the twig at the leaf scar; pith chambered; lateral buds much smaller than the terminal buds. *Liriodendron tulipifera*, tulip tree.

51b. Ringlike stipule scar described above is not present; pith is not chambered; lateral buds are not much smaller than the terminal buds. *Carya spp.*, the hickories. See chapter 8.

52a. Ringlike stipule scars encircle the twigs at the leaf scars; buds with only one scale that covers the entire bud like a hood; smooth bark peels off in large, irregular blocks; underbark yellowish and whitish. The distinctive bark with very large white, yellowish, tan, and gray splotches makes this tree easy to spot from long distances. *Platanus occidentalis*, sycamore.

52b. Ringlike stipule scars absent; bark various, but not with large areas of white, yellow, tan, and gray colors. Go to 53.

53a. Shrub with a U-shaped leaf scar that surrounds small buds; twigs red-hairy. *Rhus spp.*, the sumacs. See chapter 8.

Note: Poison oak (*Toxicodendron vernix*) resembles these species and should not be handled. It can be differentiated from the sumacs by its lateral buds, which are not surrounded by leaf scars, and by the white berries that might be present during winter.

53b. Sapling or tree with oval or shield-shaped leaf scars. Go to 54.

54a. Twigs thick; leaf scars large and shield-shaped, partially surrounding the buds; buds small and brown-hairy; many bundle scars, nine or more. *Ailanthus altissima,* tree of heaven.

54b. Twigs thin; leaf scars smaller and oval-shaped; buds not brown-hairy; fewer bundle scars. Go to 55.

55a. Buds with two to three scales. Go to 57.

55b. Buds with five to six scales. Go to 56.

56a. Twigs hairless; buds small and pressed against the twig. *Morus alba,* white mulberry.

56b. Twigs slightly hairy; buds larger and angled away from the twig. *Morus rubra,* red mulberry.

57a. Typically more than three bundle scars; pith round in cross section; bark smooth. *Tilia americana,* American basswood.

57b. Sometimes only three bundle scars; pith star-shaped in cross section, five-pointed; bark of older individuals typically deeply furrowed. Go to 58.

58a. Buds mostly downy or hairy. *Castanea pumila,* Eastern chinquapin.

58b. Buds mostly hairless. *Castanea dentata,* American chestnut.

Chapter 8

Winter Keys to Selected Genera

These keys feature species that are not included in the winter keys in chapter 7. For example, several species of *Prunus* are covered in chapter 7 because their features are easily seen. Those with less obvious features are listed under their genera in the keys below.

Amelanchier spp., Juneberries or serviceberries

1a. Tall shrub or small tree growing to 20 feet, sometimes in a clump. These two species are difficult to distinguish in the winter. *Amelanchier canadensis,* oblong-leaf serviceberry, and *Amelanchier intermedia,* swamp serviceberry.

1b. Small shrubs growing to 5 feet (usually less) in patches, spreading from underground runners. There are two species, which are difficult to distinguish in the winter. *Amelanchier obovalis,* coastal serviceberry, and *Amelanchier stolonifera,* running serviceberry.

Aronia spp., chokeberries

1a. Twigs and buds with a light-colored wool; fruit red. *Aronia arbutifolia,* red chokeberry.

1b. Twigs and buds slightly wooly, if at all. There are two species found in the Pine Barrens, *Aronia atropurpurea* and the more common *Aronia melanocarpa.* Both are called "purple chokeberries."

Betula spp., birches

1a. Bark shaggy, peeling off in thin rolls, and varying from reddish or greenish tan to brown; often with multiple trunks. *Betula nigra,* river birch.

1b. Bark whitish, not peeling as above, and not shaggy. Go to 2.

2a. Twigs reddish and warty; buds not gummy; trunks commonly have dark chevrons (sergeant's stripes) at base of branches. *Betula populifolia,* gray birch.

2b. Twigs densely hairy; buds gummy; chevrons fewer or absent. *Betula alba,* European white birch.

Carya spp., hickories

1a. End buds yellow with paired scales. Common in the Pine Barrens. *Carya cordiformis,* bitternut hickory.

1b. End buds not yellow; scales not paired but several overlapping. Go to 2.

2a. End buds mostly under ½ inch long. Go to 5.

2b. End buds mostly over ½ inch long. Go to 3.

3a. Older bark shaggy and peeling away from the tree in long strips. An introduced species that is rare in the Pine Barrens. *Carya ovata,* shagbark hickory.

3b. Older bark not as above but smooth, furrowed, or grooved and adhering to the tree. The following species are common in the Pine Barrens. Go to 4.

4a. Twigs thick and wooly or hairy; end buds to 1 inch long. *Carya tomentosa,* mockernut hickory.

4b. Twigs slender and hairless; end buds to ½ inch long, most smaller. *Carya glabra,* pignut hickory.

5a. End buds to ½ inch long; twigs and branches hairless. Common in the Pine Barrens. *Carya glabra*, pignut hickory.

5b. End buds typically to ¼ inch long. These two species are rare in the Pine Barrens. Go to 6.

6a. Older bark sometimes shaggy and peeling away from the tree in small plates or scales. *Carya ovalis*, red hickory.

6b. Older bark furrowed and not peeling away as above. *Carya pallida*, sand hickory.

Gaylussacia spp., huckleberries

1a. Shrub to 6 feet tall, often at least 3 feet; twigs with few if any hairs; leaf buds with four to five scales. *Gaylussacia frondosa*, dangleberry or tall huckleberry.

1b. Shrub typically under 3 feet; twigs hairy. Go to 2.

2a. Height to 3 feet; lateral buds with two to three scales. *Gaylussacia baccata*, black huckleberry.

2b. Height under 2 feet, typically less; lateral buds with four to five scales. *Gaylussacia dumosa*, dwarf huckleberry.

Populus spp., poplars

1a. Twigs and buds with white down or hairs; bark grayish or whitish when young but darker near the base of the tree. *Populus alba*, white poplar.

1b. Twigs mostly hairless (some may be slightly hairy); bark grayish, often with a greenish tinge. Go to 2.

2a. Buds gray or dull brown, and hairy. *Populus grandidentata*, big-toothed aspen.

2b. Buds reddish brown and glossy. *Populus tremuloides*, trembling or quaking aspen.

Prunus spp., cherries and plums

1a. Some of the shorter branches, especially the lower ones, have a pointed tip and are modified into thorns or spikes. *Prunus americana*, American plum.

1b. Branches not modified into thorns. Go to 2.

2a. Tree or sapling; true end buds; twigs and end buds mostly hairless. *Prunus serotina*, wild black cherry (Fig. 6).

2b. Low, branched shrub; false end buds; twigs and end buds hairy. *Prunus maritima*, beach plum.

Quercus spp., the oaks

The oaks are a large genus, one in which some species closely resemble others. Some individuals are difficult to place in a species even in the summer when leaves are present. In the winter, these problems become magnified. One feature that may help you is that the oaks retain dead leaves over winter. If you can find leaves that are not too badly battered, use these and the summer key. In other cases, you will have to rely on the following key. Draw some solace from the knowledge that you are not alone. Even experts do not always agree on what to call individual oaks for two reasons. First, some individuals are just ambiguous. Some features may point to one species while others seem to suggest a different one. Second, some of these ambiguities occur because different species of oaks hybridize. Either our species concept does not work well for the oaks, or even the oaks are not sure to which species they belong.

1a. Growth form tall, straight, and "treelike" with one or several more or less straight trunks. Go to 4.

1b. Growth form "shrublike," or scrubby, with twisted trunks and branches; height typically under 10 feet, normally less. Go to 2.

2a. End buds pointed and sharp, the largest longer than 3⁄16 inch, slightly angled; buds with rusty brown hairs and oval, shaped; branches thick. *Quercus marilandica*, black jack oak.

2b. End buds dull with a rounded or slightly pointed tip, the largest shorter than 3⁄16 inch and not angled. Go to 3.

3a. Buds pointed but not sharp; twigs velvety or hairy; bark greenish brown and smooth when young, becoming slightly scaly with age; leaves lobed with bristle tips. A common scrubby oak. *Quercus ilicifolia*, scrub or bear oak.

3b. Buds with rounded tip; twigs smooth and light orange-brown or red-brown; bark thin, scaly, and light brown; leaves with three to seven pairs of rounded teeth lacking bristle tips. An uncommon scrubby oak. *Quercus prinoides*, dwarf or dwarf chestnut oak.

4a. End buds hairless. Go to 9.

4b. End buds hairy, in some cases hairy only at tip. Go to 5.

5a. End buds rounded. Go to 6.

5b. End buds sharp-pointed. Go to 7.

6a. Branches stout, mostly reddish brown hairy, especially when young; bud scales dark brown; buds with sparse down; leaves deeply and regularly lobed with bristle tips. *Quercus stellata*, post oak.

6b. Branches slender; young branches may be slightly hairy; bud scales reddish brown; buds white downy above middle; leaves irregularly lobed, often cross-shaped and without bristle tips. *Quercus coccinea*, scarlet oak.

7a. End buds less than 3⁄16 inch long; leaves very deeply lobed; the three end lobes are long and slender, while the lobes at the base of the leaf are smaller. Leaves near the top of the tree look like birds' feet because of the three very prominent lobes toward the end of the leaf. *Quercus falcata*, Spanish or Southern red oak (Fig. 66).

7b. End buds 3⁄16 inch or longer. Go to 8.

8a. Older bark has deep fissures or grooves (sometimes an inch deep on older trees); inner bark not yellowish; buds downy-hairy toward tips with dark brown scales; branches mostly smooth; leaves with eight or more pairs of rounded teeth that do not end with a bristle tip. *Quercus prinus*, chestnut oak.

8b. Older bark dark and blocky, inner bark orange and not deeply furrowed as above; buds densely wooly-hairy with grayish scales; branches may be hairy; leaves typically moderately lobed with lobes ending in a bristle tip. *Quercus velutina*, black oak.

9a. End buds rounded and dull. Go to 10.

9b. End buds narrow and sharp. Go to 11.

10a. Bark light grayish (ash-colored) and forming thin, rectangular scales or flakes, less frequently furrowed; branches turn pearly gray with age; leaves have regular lobes that resemble a sergeant's stripes but with more chevrons. A common tree of uplands or transitional areas. *Quercus alba*, white oak (Fig. 14).

10b. Bark light, but usually more furrowed; branches turn reddish brown with age; leaves have irregular teeth or shallow lobes, typically fewer than six pairs. A rare tree of wetlands. *Quercus bicolor,* swamp white or swamp oak.

11a. End buds under 3⁄16 inch and angled; bud scales paler at the margin; leaves elliptical and very narrow, base and tip tapering, and with a smooth edge (lacking teeth and lobes and looking "willowlike"). *Quercus phellos,* willow oak.

11b. End buds over 3⁄16 inch and not angled; leaves with shallow teeth. Go to 12.

12a. Bark thick and dark brown, older bark with deep fissures or grooves (sometimes an inch deep on older trees). *Quercus prinus,* chestnut oak.

12b. Bark thin, scaly, and light gray. *Quercus michauxii,* basket oak.

Robinia spp., the locusts

Note the two thorns flanking the leaf scar.

1a. Small tree or shrub with weak thorns and bristly twigs and branches. *Robinia hispida,* bristly locust or rose acacia.

1b. Twigs and branches not bristly. Go to 2.

2a. Thorns usually under ½ inch long; twigs with sticky rounded structures (glands). *Robinia viscosa,* clammy locust.

2b. Thorns usually over ½ inch long; twigs without sticky glands. *Robinia pseudo-acacia,* black locust.

Rosa spp., the roses

The roses represent a challenge to the amateur and to the professional botanist even in the summer. Botanists cannot agree on the species and, apparently, neither can the roses, since cultivated varieties hybridize with wild groups. Furthermore, many once popular varieties have been planted in cemeteries, whence they have escaped to become established in the wild. The four species that I have included make up only a few of the common types, and the features I have listed in this key are not as reliable as I would have liked. The safest bet is to make a guess at an identification, knowing that your decision is likely to be more of the former than the latter.

1a. Thorns stout at base (length of base where it adheres to the stem at least one-third the length of the thorn from base to tip). Go to 3.

1b. Thorns thin and not stout at base (base length less than a quarter of the length of the thorn). Go to 2.

2a. Thorns straight; oldest stems have few, mostly weak prickles; thorns thin but wider than below (length of thorn about four times length of base); thorns flattened at base. *Rosa virginiana*, Virginia rose.

2b. Some thorns slightly curved downwards; oldest stems have few, mostly weak prickles; thorns very thin (length of thorn more than seven times length of base); thorns flattened at base. *Rosa carolina*, Carolina or pasture rose.

3a. Base of thorns stout (length of base almost equal to length of thorn); most thorns, except perhaps those on the oldest branches, curved downwards; some thorns paired. The common rose found in both wet and dry areas. *Rosa multiflora*, multiflora rose.

3b. Base of thorns less stout (base of thorn about one-third the length of the thorn); thorns of young branches curved downwards, the others straight; most thorns paired. Typically found in wet areas. *Rosa palustris*, swamp rose.

Rubus spp., blackberries and dewberries

This is another member of the rose family, with many species that are difficult to identify, even for experts and even in the summer. The two main groups are the low-running dewberries and the upright blackberries, which may have arching canes. The latter are particularly confusing. The species listed below are the most common in the Pine Barrens.

1a. Growth form upright with canes mostly erect, sometimes arching over. The blackberries. — Go to 3.

1b. Growth form mostly flattened and growing close to the ground. The dewberries. — Go to 2.

2a. Scattered, stout prickles. — *Rubus flagellaris*, prickly or Northern dewberry.

2b. Densely bristly—covered with stiff, hairlike bristles rather than prickles. — *Rubus hispidus*, bristly dewberry.

3a. Very prickly, typically with pale, curved prickles that can be as long as ½ inch; common. — *Rubus cuneifolius*, sand blackberry.

3b. Scattered, stout, mostly straight prickles. — Go to 4.

Note: These last two species are difficult to distinguish.

4a. Mature canes purplish; leaf stems prickly (see if you can find an old leaf). — *Rubus allegheniensis*, Allegheny blackberry.

4b. Mature canes not as above; leaf stems hairy rather than prickly. — *Rubus pensilvanicus*, Pennsylvania blackberry.

Smilax spp., greenbriers

1a. Leaves thick, leathery, and persistent over winter; vines climbing and rarely forming dense tangles. A greenbrier of wetlands. *Smilax laurifolia*, laurel greenbrier.

1b. Leaves thin and not persistent; vines climbing and running on the ground, sometimes forming dense tangles. Go to 2.

2a. Berries red. An uncommon greenbrier in the Pine Barrens. *Smilax walteri*, redberry greenbrier.

2b. Berries purple or black. Common greenbriers. Go to 3.

3a. Thorns present opposite joints where smaller branches separate from the main stem; young stems with a white bloom. *Smilax glauca*, glaucous greenbrier.

3b. Thorns absent from the joints where smaller branches separate from the main stem; young stems do not have a whitish bloom. *Smilax rotundifolia*, round leaf greenbrier.

Vaccinium spp., blueberries

1a. Plants are typically tall shrubs (commonly 3–10 feet tall); twigs may be short but sometimes as long as 1 foot or more and very straight. Highbush blueberries, typically found in wetlands or moist woods. Go to 2.

1b. Plants typically short, under 2 feet, and often under 1 foot tall; twigs never long and straight. Lowbush blueberries, typically found in dry woods. Go to 3.

2a. Twigs hairless or slightly hairy; young branches green, sometimes also reddish. The common blueberry of wetlands. *Vaccinium corymbosum*, common highbush blueberry.

2b. Twigs very hairy; young branches green. A rare blueberry of wetlands. *Vaccinium atrococcum*, black highbush blueberry.

3a. Young branches not grooved but distinctly warty. The common lowbush blueberry of uplands. *Vaccinium vacillans*, early lowbush blueberry.

3b. Young branches sometimes grooved and with many fine twigs; less evidently warty than above. A rarer lowbush blueberry, which typically forms dense clumps. *Vaccinium angustifolium*, late lowbush blueberry.

Viburnum spp., arrowwoods

The arrowwoods are difficult to identify in the winter. Look for dead leaves at the base of the plant and use the summer key to increase your chances of success.

1a. Lateral and terminal buds have only two scales; buds very long and slender, at least five times longer than wide. Go to 3.

1b. Lateral and sometimes terminal buds have more than two scales, although the two lowest pairs are quite small; buds slender, but not so long and thin as above. The most common species of the Pine Barrens is in this group. Go to 2.

2a. Twigs slightly ridged. This is the common arrowwood of wetlands. *Viburnum dentatum*, Southern arrowwood.

2b. Twigs mostly not ridged. *Viburnum acerifolium*, mapleleaf viburnum.

3a. End buds very long (up to ½ inch) and brownish pink in color; the slightly swollen flower buds have two scales, which do not quite meet in the center, giving those buds the appearance of a bird's head. *Viburnum nudum*, Southern wild raisin (Fig. 39).

3b. End buds shorter, reddish brown or purple, slightly hairy. *Viburnum prunifolium*, blackhaw.

Vitis spp., grapes

1a. Tendrils (or fruit or flower clusters) opposite almost every leaf scar. Go to 2.

1b. Tendrils (or fruit or flower clusters) absent from every third leaf scar. Go to 3.

2a. Twigs red and hairy. *Vitis lambrusca*, fox grape.

2b. Twigs either hairless or with scattered patches of whitish hairs. *Vitis novae-angliae*, New England grape.

3a. Pith brownish and hollow except for woody partitions or plates opposite each leaf scar; woody partitions thin, usually under 1 mm (1⁄16 inch) thick. *Vitis riparia*, riverbank grape.

3b. Woody partitions described above are thick, more than 2 mm (about ⅛ inch). Go to 4.

4a. Twigs initially red and hairy, becoming whitish and sometimes hairless with age. *Vitis aestivalis*, summer grape.

4b. Twigs hairless; fruit sometimes persists over winter. *Vitis vulpina*, frost grape.

Chapter 9

Quick Keys to Genera

This key can be used for several purposes. Use it if you are familiar with the local plants and can quickly identify key features. You can also use it to double-check an identification because much of the key is arranged differently from the more comprehensive keys that appear earlier in the text. Once you have identified a genus, look it up in the index and identify the species using the relevant sections of the text.

H. Key to the Quick Keys

1a. Plants with needlelike, nail-like, or scalelike leaves. Use key I.

1b. Plants with broad leaves or no leaves. Go to 2.

2a. Summer Keys Go to 3.

2b. Winter Keys Go to 7.

3a. Plants with opposite branching. Use key J.

3b. Plants with alternate branching. Go to 4.

4a. Plants with alternate, compound leaves. Use key K.

4b. Plants with alternate, simple leaves. Go to 5.

5a. Vines or low creeping plants under 4 inches high, including those that form mats and solitary plants arising from runners. Use key L.

5b. Trees and shrubs, the latter taller than 4 inches. Go to 6.

6a. Alternate-leaved trees and shrubs with one bundle scar. — Use key M.

6b. Alternate-leaved trees and shrubs with three or more bundle scars. — Use key N.

7. Winter Keys to the broad-leaved plants.

7a. Leaves persist over winter. — Use key O.

7b. Leaves do not persist over winter, although a few dead leaves may be found. — Go to 8.

8a. Leaf scars opposite. — Use key P.

8b. Leaf scars alternate. — Go to 9.

9a. Climbing or sprawling vines (including canes with thorns), all with alternate leaf scars. — Use key Q.

9b. Upright trees or shrubs with alternate leaf scars. — Go to 10.

10a. Three or fewer bundle scars. — Go to 11.

10b. More than three bundle scars. — Use key R.

11a. One bundle scar. — Use key S.

11b. Three bundle scars. — Go to 12.

12a. True end buds. — Use key T.

12b. False end buds. — Use key U.

I. Summer and Winter Keys to Plants with Needlelike, Nail-like, or Scalelike Leaves

1a. Plants with nail-like or scalelike leaves. Go to 2.

1b. Plants with needlelike leaves. *Pinus spp.*, the pines.

2a. Plants with some scalelike leaves. Go to 3.

2b. Plants with nail-like leaves. Go to 4.

3a. Twigs bearing scalelike leaves form a flattened spray. *Chamaecyparis thyoides*, Atlantic white cedar.

3b. Twigs more square in cross section; nail-like leaves may also be present. *Juniperus virginiana*, red cedar.

4a. Plants form mats on the surface of the ground; leaves on stems. Go to 5.

4b. Plants are low shrubs up to 6 inches tall, growing in scattered clumps rather than mats; leaves do not have leaf stems. *Hudsonia spp.*, the false heathers.

5a. Leaves appear opposite, often in whorls of three or four; leaves have minute teeth. *Corema conradii*, broom crowberry.

5b. Leaves clearly alternate and without minute teeth. *Pyxidantera barbulata*, pyxie moss.

J. Summer Key to Plants with Opposite Leaves

1a. Leaves compound. Go to 2.

1b. Leaves simple. Go to 3.

2a. Twigs warty, thick with a large pith, and lacking an end bud. *Sambucus canadensis,* common elderberry.

2b. Twigs smooth, thick with a small pith, and having a true end bud. *Fraxinus pennsylvanicus,* green ash.

3a. Plants grow as low, creeping shrubs. Go to 4.

3b. Plants are trees or shrubs. Go to 5.

4a. A small, delicate plant of wetlands with mostly hairless leaves and twigs. *Mitchella repens,* partridge berry.

4b. A sprawling, dense plant of uplands; leaves and twigs densely hairy. *Lonicera japonica,* Japanese honeysuckle.

5a. Leaves lobed. Go to 6.

5b. Leaves not lobed. Go to 7.

6a. Leaf undersides hairy; a rare shrub. *Viburnum acerifolium,* mapleleaf viburnum.

6b. Leaf undersides not hairy; trees. *Acer spp.*, the maples.

7a. Leaves large and heart-shaped, with more than three bundle scars. Go to 8.

7b. Leaves small, with three or fewer bundle scars. Go to 9.

One species may be found around abandoned houses. *Syringia vulgaris,* lilac, has small, heart-shaped leaves.

8a. Pith solid; leaves sometimes in threes. *Catalpa speciosa,* common catalpa.

8b. Pith chambered; leaves never in threes. *Paulownia tomentosa,* princess tree.

9a. Leaves very small and leathery, sometimes alternate on a low shrub; leaves never in threes. A rare plant. *Leiophyllum buxifolium*, sand myrtle.

9b. Leaves larger, not leathery, and either in pairs or threes but never alternate. Go to 10.

10a. Leaves sometimes in threes. Go to 11.

10b. Leaves never in threes. Go to 12.

11a. A small shrub with distinctive light green leaves; lateral veins on leaves indistinct. *Kalmia angustifolia*, sheep laurel.

11b. A tall shrub near water with distinctive hard, round fruit; lateral veins distinct and tending to follow leaf outline. *Cephalanthus occidentalis*, buttonbush.

12a. One bundle scar. Go to 15.

12b. Three bundle scars. Go to 13.

13a. Lateral veins of leaves follow, running almost parallel to, leaf edge; leaf edge smooth. *Cornus florida*, flowering dogwood.

13b. Lateral veins of leaves break up before reaching edge of leaf; leaves toothed or wavy-edged. Go to 14.

14a. Branchlets hollow; bud scales remain to mark border between branchlet and twig. *Lonicera tatarica*, Tartarian honeysuckle.

14b. Branchlets not hollow. *Viburnum spp.*, the arrowwoods.

15a. Small shrubs with very small buds, the latter with two scales; leaves small and elongate (at least four times longer than wide). *Hypericum spp.*, the St. Johnsworts and related species.

15b. Tall shrubs or small trees having buds with more than two scales and leaves that are more elliptical (two to three times longer than wide). Go to 16.

16a. Leaves small, under 3 inches; twigs slender; leaf scar raised. A common escapee. *Ligustrum vulgare*, common privet.

16b. Leaves large, typically 4 inches or more; twigs thicker; leaf scar not raised. A rare shrub. *Chionanthus virginicus*, fringe tree.

K. Summer Key to the Plants with Alternate, Compound Leaves

1a. Leaves once compound. Go to 3.

1b. Leaves twice compound. Go to 2.

2a. Thorns present. *Gleditsia trianthos*, honey locust.

2b. Thorns absent. *Albizzia julibrissin*, albizzia.

3a. Thorns present. Go to 4.

3b. Thorns absent. Go to 6.

4a. Upright trees. *Robinia spp.*, the locusts.

4b. Climbing or sprawling vines or canes. Go to 5.

5a. Stipules connect leaf bases to stems. *Rosa spp.*, the roses.

5b. Leaf bases do not have stipules attaching to the stems. *Rubus spp.*, blackberries and dewberries.

6a. Three leaflets; hairy vines or shrubs. *Toxicodendron spp.*, poison ivy and oak.

6b. More than three leaflets. Go to 7.

7a. Climbing or sprawling vines. Go to 8.

7b. Upright trees or shrubs. Go to 9.

8a. Five leaflets, all arising from a central point at the end of the leaf stem. *Parthenocissus quinquefolia*, Virginia creeper.

8b. More than five leaflets, more or less in pairs arising from many points along the leaf stem. *Wisteria sinensis*, wisteria.

9a. Three leaflets or with simple leaves; a sprawling shrub with very slender, grooved, green stems. *Cytisus scoparius*, Scotch broom.

9b. More than three leaflets. Go to 10.

10a. Pith chambered; bundle scars in groups of three circles or *U*'s. *Juglans nigra*, black walnut.

10b. Pith not chambered. Go to 11.

11a. Buds very small, often hidden; twigs and branches hairy and slender; shrubs. *Rhus spp.*, the sumacs.

11b. Buds and twigs larger; trees. Go to 12.

12a. False end buds; leaves with many leaflets, often more than twenty. *Ailanthus altissima*, tree of heaven.

12b. True end buds; leaves with fewer than twenty leaflets. *Carya spp.*, the hickories.

L. Summer Key to Alternate-Leaved Plants That Grow as Vines, Form Mats, or Arise from Underground Runners

1a. Vines and plants trailing or forming dense mats. Go to 3.

1b. Scattered plants under 4 inches high, arising from underground runners but not forming mats. Go to 2.

2a. Leaves coarse-toothed with few teeth. *Chimaphila spp.*, princess pine and spotted wintergreen.

2b. Leaves with many minute teeth or not toothed; crushed leaves smell of teaberry. *Gaultheria procumbens*, teaberry.

3a. Thorns present. *Smilax spp.*, greenbriers.

3b. Thorns absent. Go to 4.

4a. Vines that climb using tendrils. *Vitis spp.*, the grapes.

4b. Vines or mat-forming plants without tendrils. Go to 5.

5a. Large heart-shaped, hairy leaves. *Epigaea repens*, Mayflower or trailing arbutus.

5b. Leaves smaller than 1 inch long. Go to 6.

6a. A plant of wet depressions, mostly forming mats or low tangles. *Vaccinium macrocarpon*, cranberry.

6b. A plant of upland areas, mostly trailing. *Arctostaphylos uva-ursi*, bearberry.

M. Summer Key to Alternate-Leaved Shrubs and Trees with One Bundle Scar

1a. End buds clustered with one large flower bud and several much smaller flower buds. Leaf edges lack teeth but have tiny hairs along the edge. *Rhododendron spp.*, the azaleas.

1b. End buds single, leaf edges various. Go to 2.

2a. True end buds. Go to 8.

2b. False endbuds. Go to 3.

3a. Twigs and branches densely covered with many very tiny white dots. *Vaccinium spp.*, the blueberries.

3b. Twigs and branches not covered as above, although larger scattered dots, silvery or brown scales, or lenticels may be present. Go to 4.

4a. Leaf undersides and sometimes upper surfaces covered by yellow resin droplets. *Gaylussacia spp.*, the huckleberries.

4b. Leaf undersides do not have liquid-looking resin droplets, although brownish scales may be present.

5a. Upper and lower surfaces of leaves covered with brown or silvery scales; clusters of flower buds present; a small shrub, often growing in dense stands in very wet areas. *Chamaedaphne calyculata*, leatherleaf.

5b. Upper and lower surfaces not so covered. Go to 6.

6a. Pith chambered; buds small and dark with two scales; leaves not toothed; a small tree with distinctive blocky bark. *Diospyros virginiana*, persimmon.

6b. Shrubs often have capsules; pith not chambered; bark not distinctively blocky; leaves toothed or not. Go to 7.

7a. Slender spikes of reddish or greenish flower buds usually present; capsules fragile when open; leaves toothed and long-pointed. *Leucothoe racemosa*, swamp sweetbells.

7b. Slender spikes of flower buds not present; capsules woody when open, either urn-shaped or round; buds sometimes reddish; leaves toothed or not, not long-pointed. *Lyonia spp.*, maleberry and staggerbush.

8. Alternate-leaved plants with true end buds and one bundle scar.

8a. Twigs and undersides of leaves covered with brown and silvery scales; undersides of leaves are distinctly metallic-silvery. *Elaeagnus spp.*, the "olives."

8b. Twigs and leaves not as above. Go to 9.

9a. Leaves toothed, even if only a few teeth at the tip, or leaves have spikelike extensions. Go to 11.

9b. Leaves not toothed. Go to 10.

10a. Leaves slightly thickened and leathery. *Kalmia latifolia*, mountain laurel.

10b. Leaves not thickened. *Nemopanthus mucronatus*, catberry.

11a. Small, dark, spikelike stipules or dark, triangular stipule scars flank the leaf scars and leaf bases; end buds about the same size as lateral buds; fruit a berry. *Ilex spp.*, the hollies and inkberries.

11b. Stipules absent; end buds much larger than lateral buds; lowest two bud scales long and fleshy; clusters of fragile capsules often present. *Clethra alnifolia,* sweet pepperbush.

N. Upright Shrubs and Trees with Three or More Bundle Scars

1a. End buds clustered. Go to 2.

1b. End buds single, not clustered. Go to 3.

2a. Shrubs with small buds having indistinct scales; leaves have three lobes and rounded teeth on the lobes. *Hibiscus syriacus,* rose of Sharon.

2b. Mostly trees but a few shrubs having large buds with distinct scales; leaves mostly lobed or coarse-toothed (not with three lobes and rounded teeth on the lobes). *Quercus spp.*, the oaks.

3a. True end buds. Go to 14.

3b. False end buds. Go to 4.

4a. Leaves very long and narrow with rounded, sometimes pointed teeth or lobes along the edges, often with yellow resin dots; crushed leaves have a pleasant, spicy smell. *Comptonia peregrina,* sweet fern.

4b. Leaves lack the above combination of features. Go to 5.

5a. Thorns present. *Crataegus uniflora*, dwarf hawthorn.

5b. Thorns absent. Go to 6.

6a. At least some leaves lobed. Go to 7.

6b. Leaves not lobed. Go to 8.

7a. Leaves symmetrical with five lobes and spiky teeth; bark peeling and smooth with large areas of gray, white, and tan blotches. *Platanus occidentalis*, sycamore.

7b. Leaves asymmetrically lobed; both lobed and nonlobed leaves, these having teeth that do not end in spikes; bark furrowed. *Morus spp.*, the mulberries.

8a. Leaf scars with only three bundle scars. Go to 11.

8b. Leaf scars with three or sometimes more bundle scars. Go to 9.

9a. Leaves with regular bases and coarse-toothed with well-defined lateral veins running past the ends of the teeth to form spikes. *Castanea spp.*, chestnut and dwarf chestnut.

9b. Leaves with irregular bases and not coarse-toothed as above. Go to 10.

10a. Leaf tip elongated; pith chambered. *Celtis occidentalis*, American hackberry.

10b. Leaf does not have a long point; pith not chambered. *Tilia americana*, American basswood.

11a. Crushed leaves have a pleasant, spicy smell. Go to 12.

11b. Crushed leaves do not have a pleasant, spicy smell. Go to 13.

12a. Resin dots on undersides and sometimes tops of leaves; tips of leaves have a few teeth. *Myrica spp.*, the bayberries.

12b. Leaves do not have resin dots or teeth as described above. *Lindera benzoin*, spicebush.

13a. Leaves long and slender; all leaves toothed. *Salix nigra*, black willow.

13b. Leaves not long and slender, rather two types—upper leaves elliptical and not toothed, lower leaves roughly rectangular and coarse-toothed along two sides. *Baccharis halimifolia*, groundsel tree.

14. True end buds.

14a. Leaves toothed; three bundle scars. Go to 15.

14b. Leaves not toothed; more than three bundle scars. *Magnolia virginiana*, sweetbay magnolia.

15a. Broken twigs and bruised bark have an unpleasant, bitter almond smell. *Prunus spp.*, cherries and plums.

15b. Broken twigs and bruised bark do not have this unpleasant smell. Go to 16.

16a. Lowest bud scale centered directly over leaf scar; leaf stems typically flattened. *Populus spp.*, the poplars.

16b. Lowest bud scales placed to the sides, not centrally located over leaf scars; leaf stems rounded. Go to 17.

17a. Leaves with double teeth. *Betula spp.*, the birches.

17b. Leaves do not have double teeth. Go to 18.

18a. Leaf scars often have a row of several lateral buds located above them; twigs green. *Itea virginica*, sweet spires.

18b. Only one lateral bud above leaf scars. Go to 19.

19a. Upper surface of leaves has tiny, dark, thickened hairs or glands along the central vein. *Aronia spp.*, the chokeberries.

19b. Thickened hairs or glands absent from central vein on upper surface of leaves. Go to 20.

20a. Twigs and buds hairy; short spur branches present; apples grow in summer and fall. *Pyrus malus*, the apples.

20b. Twigs and buds hairless; short spur branches not common; fruit is a sour, applelike berry. *Amelanchier spp.*, the serviceberries.

O. Broad-Leaved Plants with Green Leaves Persisting over Winter

1a. Leaves opposite or whorled. Go to 2.

1b. Leaves alternate. Go to 5.

2a. Upright shrubs. Go to 3.

2b. Low creeping shrubs or vines, the latter sometimes climbing. Go to 4.

3a. Leaves pale green and usually longer than 1 inch, sometimes appearing in whorls of three. *Kalmia angustifolia*, sheep laurel.

3b. Leaves darker and more leathery, usually shorter than ½ inch, the lower ones sometimes alternate. *Leiophyllum buxifolium*, sand myrtle.

4a. A fragile, not very woody plant growing in wetlands and having roughly heart-shaped leaves. *Mitchella repens*, partridgeberry.

4b. Twigs and leaves very hairy. *Lonicera japonica*, Japanese honeysuckle.

5a. Low creeping shrubs or vines, including very low plants with underground stems. Go to 6.

5b. Upright trees and shrubs. Go to 11.

6a. Vines with thorns. *Smilax spp.*, the greenbriers.

6b. Low creeping shrubs without thorns. Go to 7.

7a. Leaves with a few coarse teeth (and sometimes a whitish streak); stems underground. *Chimaphila spp.*, false wintergreen and princess pine.

7b. Leaves do not have coarse teeth.

8a. Crushed leaves have a pleasant, wintergreen smell; stems underground. *Gaultheria procumbens*, wintergreen.

8b. Crushed leaves do not smell of wintergreen. Go to 9.

9a. Leaves heart-shaped and hairy; stems hairy. *Epigaea repens*, Mayflower or trailing arbutus.

9b. Leaves and stems hairless; leaves not heart-shaped. Go to 10.

10a. A plant of dry uplands. *Arctostaphylos uva-ursi*, bearberry.

10b. A plant of wet depressions and wetlands. *Vaccinium macrocarpon*, cranberry.

11a. More than three bundle scars; leaves often limited to the tops of this small tree; whitened undersides of leaves visible from the ground. *Magnolia virginiana*, sweetbay magnolia.

11b. Three or fewer bundle scars; leaves not as above. Go to 12.

12a. Undersides and sometimes upper surfaces of leaves, buds, and twigs bear yellow resin dots (use hand lens). *Myrica cerifera*, wax myrtle.

12b. Resin dots absent from leaf undersides. Go to 13.

13a. Upper and lower surfaces of leaves have scattered brownish or silvery scales; clusters of flower buds present at ends of branches over winter; a small shrub, typically under 2 feet, growing in groups in or near water. *Chamaedaphne calyculata*, leatherleaf.

13b. Brownish or silvery scales absent; a taller shrub. Go to 14.

14a. Leaves either toothed at tip or with sharp spines along edges; shrubs or small trees that often grow straight rather than gnarly or twisted. *Ilex spp.*, the hollies and inkberries.

14b. Leaves without teeth or spines; gnarly, often tall shrubs. *Kalmia latifolia*, mountain laurel.

P. Plants with Opposite Leaf Scars, Leaves Not Persisting over Winter

1a. One bundle scar. Go to 2.

1b. Three or more bundle scars. Go to 5.

2a. Leaf scars sometimes whorled in threes; hard, round fruit sometimes present (about ½ inch in diameter); false end buds; a large shrub growing near water. *Cephalanthus occidentalis*, buttonbush.

2b. Leaf scars not whorled; true end buds; either a tree or small shrub. Go to 3.

3a. Small shrubs whose buds have two scales. *Hypericum spp.*, St. Johnsworts and related species.

3b. Trees and large shrubs having buds with four or more scales. Go to 4.

4a. Twigs more than ⅛ inch thick; leaf scars not raised (not common). *Chionanthus virginicus*, fringe tree.

4b. Twigs thin, less than half the thickness of the plant above; leaf scars raised. *Ligustrum vulgare*, common privet.

5a. Three bundle scars. Go to 9.

5b. More than three bundle scars. Go to 6.

6a. Leaf scars connected with a line; shrubs with pronounced lenticels. *Sambucus canadensis*, common elderberry.

6b. Leaf scars not connected with a line; trees. Go to 7.

7a. True end buds. *Fraxinus pennsylvanica*, green ash.

7b. End buds false or absent. Go to 8.

8a. Pith diaphragmed. *Paulownia tomentosa*, princess tree.

8b. Pith solid, not diaphragmed.
Catalpa speciosa, common catalpa. This species cannot be distinguished from *C. Bignonoides* without examining the flowers.

9a. Young branches hollow. *Lonicera tatarica*, Tartarian honeysuckle.

9b. Young branches solid. Go to 10.

10a. Some end buds swollen, round, and stalked; branches greenish purplish. *Cornus florida*, flowering dogwood.

10b. No end buds stalked. Go to 11.

11a. Shrubs, typically with long, slender branches; end buds may have two scales; lateral buds lie close to the twig. *Viburnum spp.*, arrowwoods.

11b. Trees, typically with some short, spurlike branches, these often with many leaf scars; lateral buds do not lie against the twig (in the most common species, distinctly reddish). *Acer spp.*, the maples.

Q. Alternate-Leaved Plants That Are Climbing or Sprawling Vines, Canes with Thorns, or Low Creeping Shrubs

1a. Sprawling or climbing vines whose stems are often covered with hairy rootlets, which help the plant climb; white berries sometimes present. *Toxicodendron radicans*, poison ivy.

1b. Other vines, canes, or creeping shrubs whose stems lack hairy rootlets. Go to 2.

2a. Low creeping shrubs, the broken bark of which smells like bitter almonds. *Prunus depressa*, sand cherry.

2b. Sprawling or climbing vines, or canes. Go to 3.

3a. Thorns present. Go to 6.

3b. Thorns absent. Go to 4.

4a. Tendrils absent, one bundle scar. *Wisteria sinensis*, wisteria.

4b. Tendrils present, bundle scars more than one or indistinct. Go to 5.

5a. Pith continuous; mostly a thin, sprawling vine that sometimes climbs. *Parthenocissus quinquefolia,* Virginia creeper.

5b. Pith has woody partitions opposite leaf scars; a thicker, climbing vine that sometimes sprawls. *Vitis spp.*, the grapes.

6a. Tendrils present. *Smilax,spp.*, the greenbriers.

6b. Tendrils absent. Go to 7.

7a. Leaf scars very narrow, with three bundle scars; swollen flower bases (or "hips") often remain on plant over winter; vines often climb. *Rosa spp.*, the roses.

7b. Leaf scars buried beneath base of leaf stems, which remain over winter, masking bundle scars; hips not present; arching canes or running stems. *Rubus spp.*, the blackberries and dewberries.

R. Upright, Alternate-Leaved Plants with Four or More Bundle Scars

1a. Clusters of white berries usually present over winter; leaf scars *U*-shaped; buds small. *Toxicodendron vernix,* poison oak.

1b. Lacking the features above. Go to 2.

2a. End buds clustered. Go to 3.

2b. End buds single, not clustered. Go to 4.

3a. End buds large, many scales evident; stipule scars absent; acorns or dried oak leaves often present; trees or gnarly shrubs. *Quercus spp.*, the oaks.

3b. End buds small, may be absent over winter; stipule scars evident and large; capsules may be present; tall shrubs or small trees. *Hibiscus syriacus*, rose of Sharon.

4a. True end buds. Go to 5.

4b. False end buds. Go to 6.

5a. Stipule scars present; pith chambered. *Liriodendron tulipifera*, tulip tree.

5b. Stipule scars absent. *Carya spp.*, the hickories.

6a. Twigs hairy; lateral buds small and indistinct, surrounded by leaf scars; shrubs. *Rhus spp.*, the sumacs.

6b. Trees with prominent lateral buds. Go to 7.

7a. Smooth bark peels, leaving large areas of white, gray, yellow, and tan blotches; buds have one scale.

7b. Does not have the above combination of traits. Go to 8.

8a. Twigs stout; leaf scars large; pith yellow; buds small. *Ailanthus altissima*, tree of heaven.

8b. Twigs more slender; leaf scars small; pith white; buds with more than four visible scales. *Morus spp.*, the mulberries.

S. Alternate-Leaved Plants with One Bundle Scar

1a. End buds clustered; shrubs. *Rhododendron spp.*, the azaleas.

1b. End buds single. Go to 2.

2a. Twigs very slender, green, and grooved; a small, delicate shrub with arching branches. *Cytisus scoparius*, Scotch broom.

2b. Does not have the above combination of traits. Go to 3.

3a. Twigs densely covered with silvery and brownish scales. *Elaeagnus spp.*, the olives.

3b. Twigs not as above. Go to 4.

4a. True end buds. Go to 5.

4b. False end buds. Go to 8.

5a. Twigs and branches green; broken bark has a pleasant, spicy smell and taste. *Sassafras albidum*, sassafras.

5b. Twigs and branches not as above. Go to 6.

6a. Small, triangular, dark brown or black stipule scars present. *Ilex spp.*, the deciduous hollies.

6b. Stipule scars described above absent. Go to 7.

7a. End buds much longer than lateral buds; end buds have two long, fleshy scales extending from the base to past the tip of the rest of the bud; clusters of fragile capsules often present over winter; common throughout the Pine Barrens. *Clethra alnifolia,* sweet pepperbush.

7b. End buds about the same size as lateral buds, all with long points; reddish fruit may be present over winter; rare, restricted to peripheral areas of the Pine Barrens. *Nemopanthus mucronatus,* mountain holly.

8a. Trees with blocky bark; chambered pith; large, fleshy fruit that has a stony pit and is dark orange when ripe. *Diospyros virginiana,* persimmon.

8b. Shrubs; pith not chambered. Go to 9.

9a. Twigs and young branches green, sometimes with reddish tinge, and densely covered with many minute white speckles. *Vaccinium spp.,* the blueberries.

9b. Twigs variously colored—if green, then limited to small areas, but not densely covered with white speckles. Go to 10.

10a. Buds along branches of two sizes, larger flower buds with four or more scales and smaller leaf buds with three or fewer scales; twigs and bud scales have a few scattered, yellow resin dots; fruit a black berry that may occasionally persist over winter. *Gaylussacia spp.,* the huckleberries.

10b. Buds along branches of one size, although a spray of flower buds may be present; resin dots absent; fruit a capsule. Go to 11.

11a. Sprays of reddish or greenish flower buds present at the tips of some twigs; open and closed capsules may also be present. *Leucothoe racemosa,* swamp sweetbells.

11b. Sprays described above are absent; hard, woody capsules with whitish streaks may be present. *Lyonia spp.,* maleberry and staggerbush.

T. Upright Plants with Alternate Leaf Scars, Three Bundle Scars, and True End Buds

1a. Pith chambered, sometimes faintly. Go to 2.

1b. Pith not chambered. Go to 4.

2a. Twigs thick; leaf scars large, with three lobes; bundle scars appear as three circles or U-shaped curves; pith open, with brownish woody partitions. *Juglans nigra,* black walnut.

2b. Pith solid, with woody diaphragms. Go to 3.

3a. Common wetland tree with many short, spikelike brown or reddish branches, which stick out at almost 90-degree angles from the main branch; one bud above the leaf scar; fruit not evident over winter. *Nyssa sylvatica,* sour gum.

3b. Rare shrub with straight, greenish branches, often with several buds in a line above the leaf scar; woody capsules sometimes present over winter. *Itea virginica,* sweet spire.

4a. Bruised bark of branches has an unpleasant, bitter almond smell. *Prunus spp.,* the cherries and plums.

4b. Bruised bark does not have an unpleasant, bitter almond smell. Go to 5.

5a. Thorns present. Go to 6.

5b. Thorns absent. Go to 7.

6a. At least a few of the thorns may have leaf scars or buds. *Malus angustifolia*, southern crab apple.

6b. No thorns have leaf scars or buds. *Crataegus uniflora*, dwarf hawthorn.

7a. Twigs and buds have small, yellow resin dots; crushed buds have pleasant, spicy smell. *Myrica spp.*, the bayberries.

7b. Twigs and buds do not have yellow resin dots; although crushed buds may have a pleasant smell, this does not resemble the smell of bayberry candles (or bay rum). Go to 8.

8a. Some branches have corky "wings" along part of their lengths; large, round, hard, thorny, ball-like fruit present over winter (and visible from the ground). *Liquidambar styraciflua*, sweetgum.

8b. Branches do not have wings; plants do not bear fruit. Go to 9.

9a. Small buds covered by one hoodlike scale; twigs very thin. *Salix nigra*, black willow.

9b. More than one bud scale. Go to 10.

10a. Lowest bud scale centered directly over leaf scar. *Populus spp.*, the poplars.

10b. Lowest bud scales positioned to the sides, flanking center of leaf scar. Go to 11.

11a. Buds stalked; hard, conelike fruit present. *Alnus serrulata*, common alder.

11b. Buds not stalked; conelike fruit not present. Go to 12.

12a. Buds with two or three scales; long, fragile, pendulous fruit sometimes persists over winter; bark smooth, often very light, with darker lateral lines. *Betula spp.*, the birches.

12b. Buds with more than three scales; plants do not bear fruit. Go to 13.

13a. Bark sinewy (like a muscle); buds often twisted and with reddish scales, the latter dark-tipped but not notched. *Amelanchier spp.*, the serviceberries.

13b. Bark not sinewy; bud scales dark-tipped and notched. *Aronia spp.*, the chokeberries.

U. Upright Plants with Alternate Leaf Scars, Three Bundle Scars, and False End Buds

1a. Thorns present; these are sometimes sharpened branches. Go to 2.

1b. Thorns absent. Go to 4.

2a. A pair of thorns flanks the leaf scars. *Robinia spp.*, the locusts.

2b. Thorns single, not flanking the leaf scars as a pair. Go to 3.

3a. Thorns are sharpened, modified branches with leaf scars and, often, buds; bruised bark has bitter almond smell. *Prunus spp.*, the plums.

3b. Thorns may be forked, do not have leaf scars or buds; bruised bark does not have unpleasant, bitter almond smell. *Gleditsia triacanthos*, honey locust.

4a. Crushed twigs have a pleasant, spicy smell. Go to 5.

4b. Crushed twigs do not have a pleasant, spicy smell. Go to 6.

5a. Twigs slender; branches, twigs, and/or buds have minute, yellow resin dots; lateral flower buds do not flank the leaf scars; a small shrub. *Comptonia peregrina*, sweet fern.

5b. Twigs not very slender; yellow resin dots absent; stalked flower buds flank some leaf scars; a large shrub or small tree that is not common. *Lindera benzoin*, spicebush.

6a. Twigs very slender, green, and clearly grooved; a small shrub often found near the bays but less commonly, inland. *Baccharis halimifolia*, groundsel tree.

6b. Twigs not very slender, green, or grooved. Go to 7.

7a. Pith usually chambered. *Celtis occidentalis*, American hackberry.

7b. Pith not chambered. Go to 8.

8a. Buds long, with many scales. *Ulmus spp.*, the elms.

8b. Buds smaller, with three or fewer scales. Go to 9.

9a. Pith round in cross section; bark smooth; buds and leaf scars small, the latter rounded; three bundle scars; a small tree that has escaped. *Albizzia julibrissin*, albizzia or mimosa.

9b. Pith angled in cross section, typically five-sided; bark furrowed; buds and leaf scars larger; leaf scars narrower than above; usually three bundle scars, sometimes more; uncommon, native woodland plant. *Castanea spp.*, American chestnut and chinquapin.

Figure 1. *Toxicodendron radicans,* poison ivy, showing leaves, fruit, and hairy stem. Learn to recognize this and poison sumac before you begin taking samples of plants. In both cases the leaves are glossy, and the plants may have white berries. In southern New Jersey, poison ivy can grow as a low vine, a climbing vine, or an upright shrub. Poison sumac is an upright shrub with compound leaves that have seven to thirteen leaflets.

Figure 2. *Pyxidanthera barbulata,* pyxie "moss." This flowering plant has nail-like leaves and forms a mat that covers the ground. The small, white flowers appear in the early spring. Magnified about two times (2x).

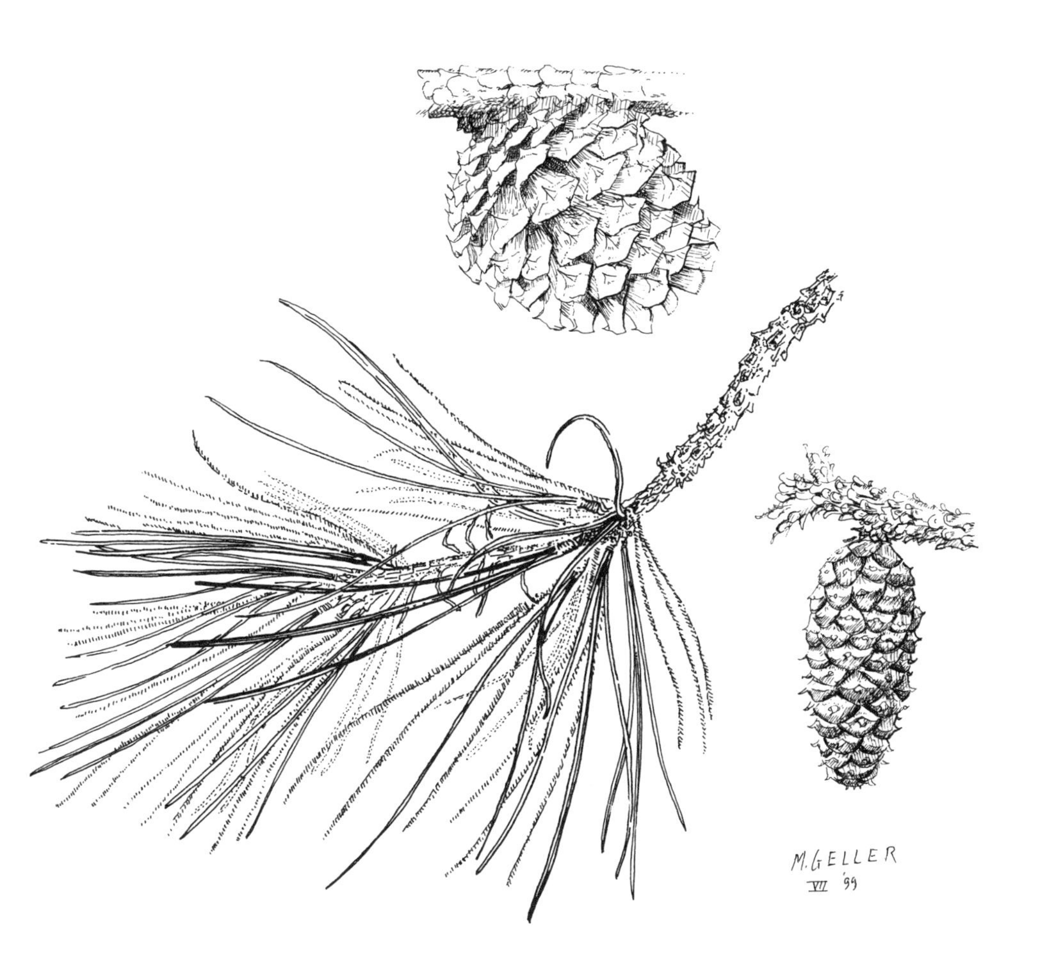

Figure 3. *Pinus rigida,* pitch pine. A plant with needlelike leaves. The cones may be open (*top*) or closed (*lower*), and on some trees the cones stay closed until they are heated by a forest fire. In both cases, the cones are armed with stout prickles.

Figure 4. *Hudsonia ericoides,* false heather. This is a flowering plant with nail-like leaves. Upper drawing is magnified about ten times (10x).

Figure 5. *Juniperus virginiana,* red cedar. On the left a twig and a portion of a branch at actual size show two types of leaves. The two views on the right have been magnified 20x. The upper shows scalelike leaves while the lower shows nail-like leaves. Both are frequently found on the same plant. *Chamaecyparis thyoides,* Atlantic white cedar, has scale-like leaves only. Its twigs form flattened sprays rather than sprays that approximate squares in cross section, which is characteristic of red cedar.

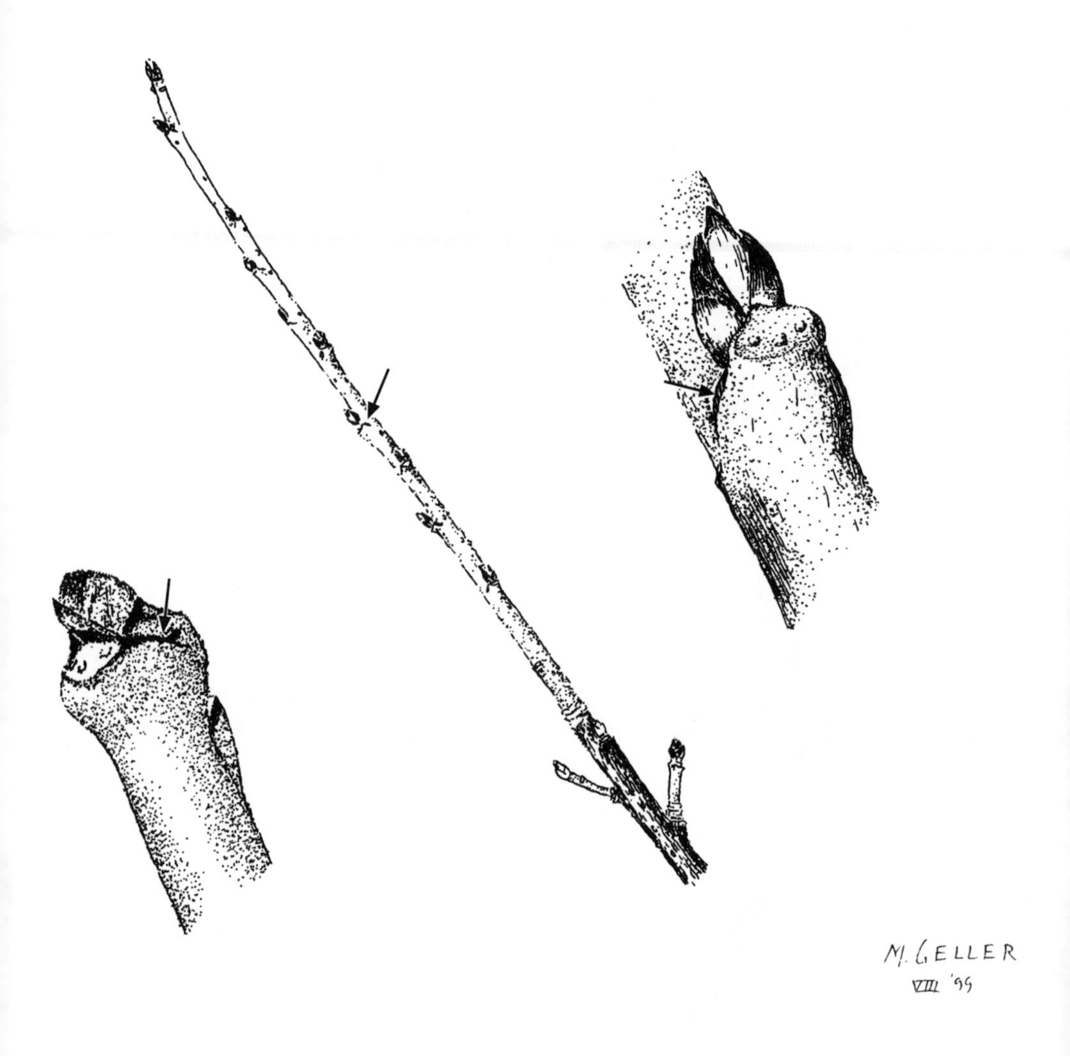

Figure 6. *Prunus serotina,* black cherry, in the leafless condition. This drawing illustrates several important features. A twig and a portion of the branch are shown in the center illustration. You can see the separation between the branchlet and the twig if you carefully examine the lower portion of this center figure (note the slight discoloration and the bands separating the two). The drawing on the left shows a 20x magnification of the true end bud. The illustration on the right is a similar view of a lateral bud. Note the overlapping bud scales in both. Below the buds are the leaf scars, and within the leaf scars are the three bundle scars. These mark where the leaf veins were attached. You can also see a small stipule scar (arrows), a feature lacking in many other species.

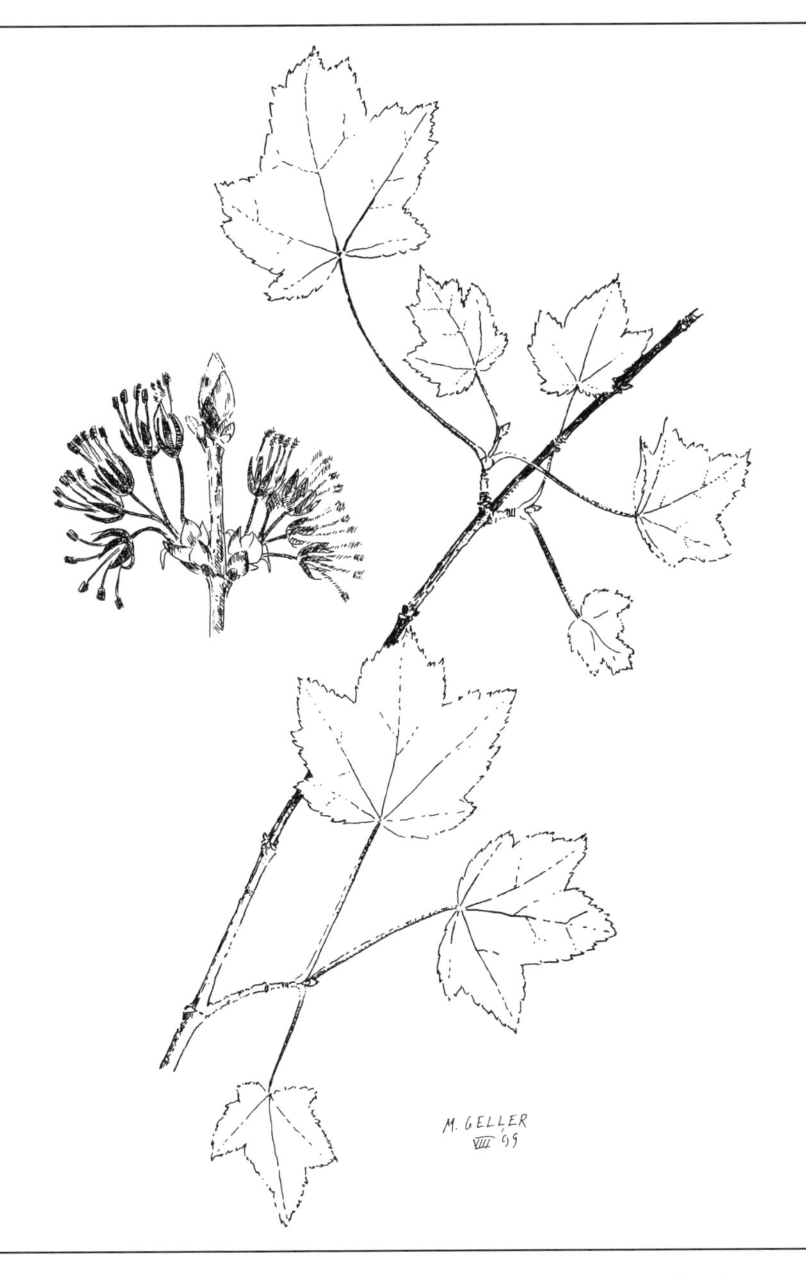

Figure 7. *Acer rubrum,* red maple. Reduced about 50% (0.5x). This plant has opposite branching. While not all branches have another branch opposite, many do. More importantly, every leaf scar has another opposite it. This plant also has lobed leaves, which show a palmate pattern of lobing. The red maple common in the Pine Barrens is a subspecies whose leaves usually have three lobes. It flowers very early in the spring with many small blossoms, giving the whole tree a slightly reddish tinge. The individual flowers are inconspicuous (top).

Figure 8. *Rhododendron spp.,* the azaleas. Reduced about 50% (0.5x). This plant has alternate branching that might appear to be opposite on first examination. Because the end buds are clustered toward the tip of the twig, several new twigs can grow from that point, making the branching pattern look opposite or whorled. However, the growth pattern is actually alternate. Note the location of the leaf scars and buds on some of the other branches. You can see that the lateral leaf scars and buds do not have an opposite branching pattern but alternate instead. The overall pattern is alternate despite what you might gather from a superficial examination. The leaves of the common wild azaleas have fine hairs along their edges (Fig. 30).

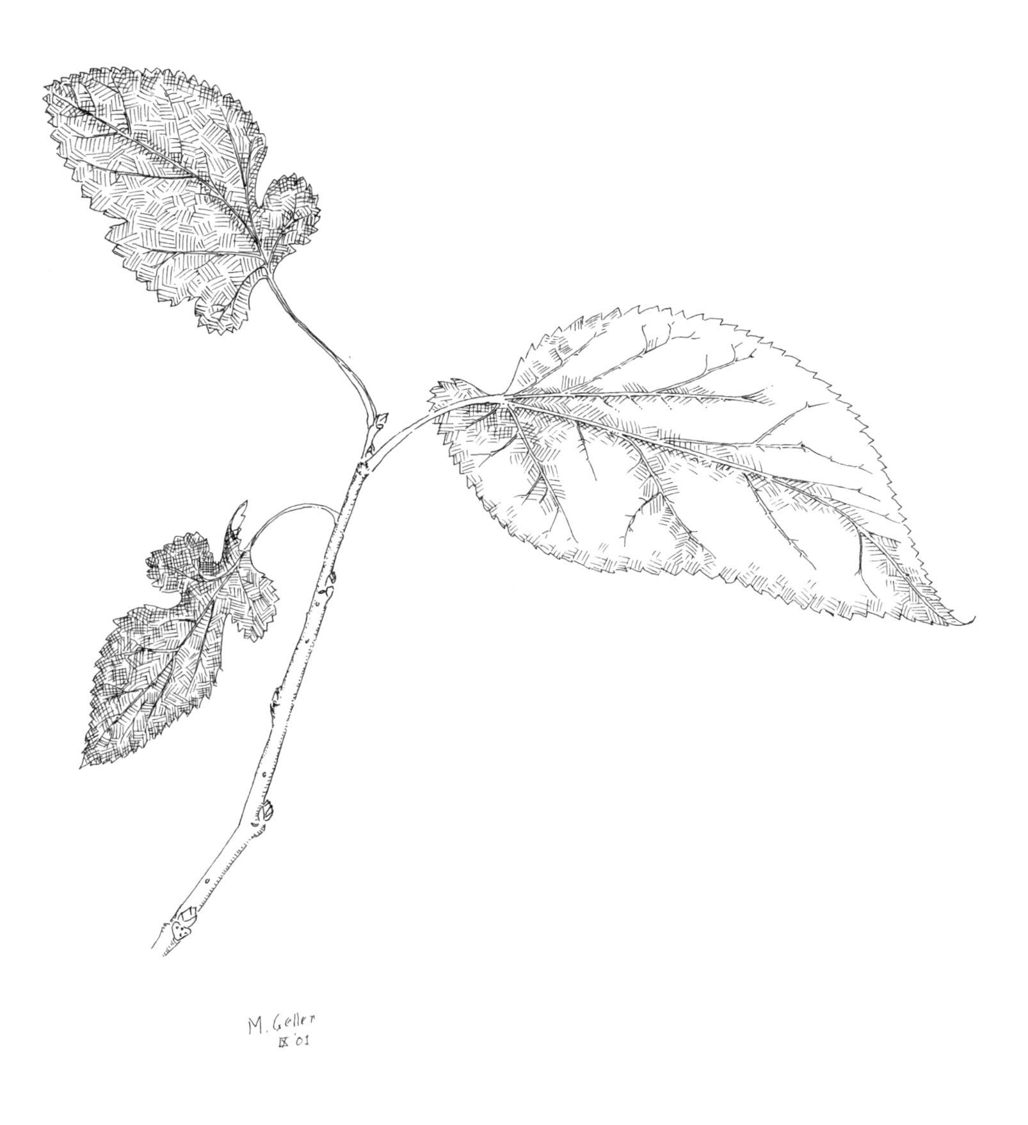

Figure 9. Lobed and nonlobed leaves of *Morus spp.,* the mulberries. These species have leaves that can be lobed or not, and as the figure shows, different kinds of leaves can be found on one plant. Often the leaves exposed to more light show greater lobing.

Figure 10. *Rhus copallina,* winged or dwarf sumac. Unlike red maple and azalea, the sumacs (and poison ivy) have compound leaves. In this case, the leaflets are in rows, not in a palmate pattern, which is seen in Figure 10. Several features help you determine whether a leaf is simple or compound (Table 2.1).

Figure 11. *Rosa multiflora,* wild rose. This shows several features. First, the plant has a compound leaf with leaflets arranged in rows. Second, thorns are evident. Depending on the plant, thorns can be modified leaves, modified twigs, or modifications of other plant parts. Third, the base of the leaf stem is modified into a stipule (arrows).

Figure 12. *Parthenocissus quinquefolia,* Virginia creeper. Another plant with a compound leaf but in this case, the leaflets are arranged in a palmate pattern.

Figure 13. *Sassafras albidum,* sassafras, illustrating the variety of leaf shapes found in this species.

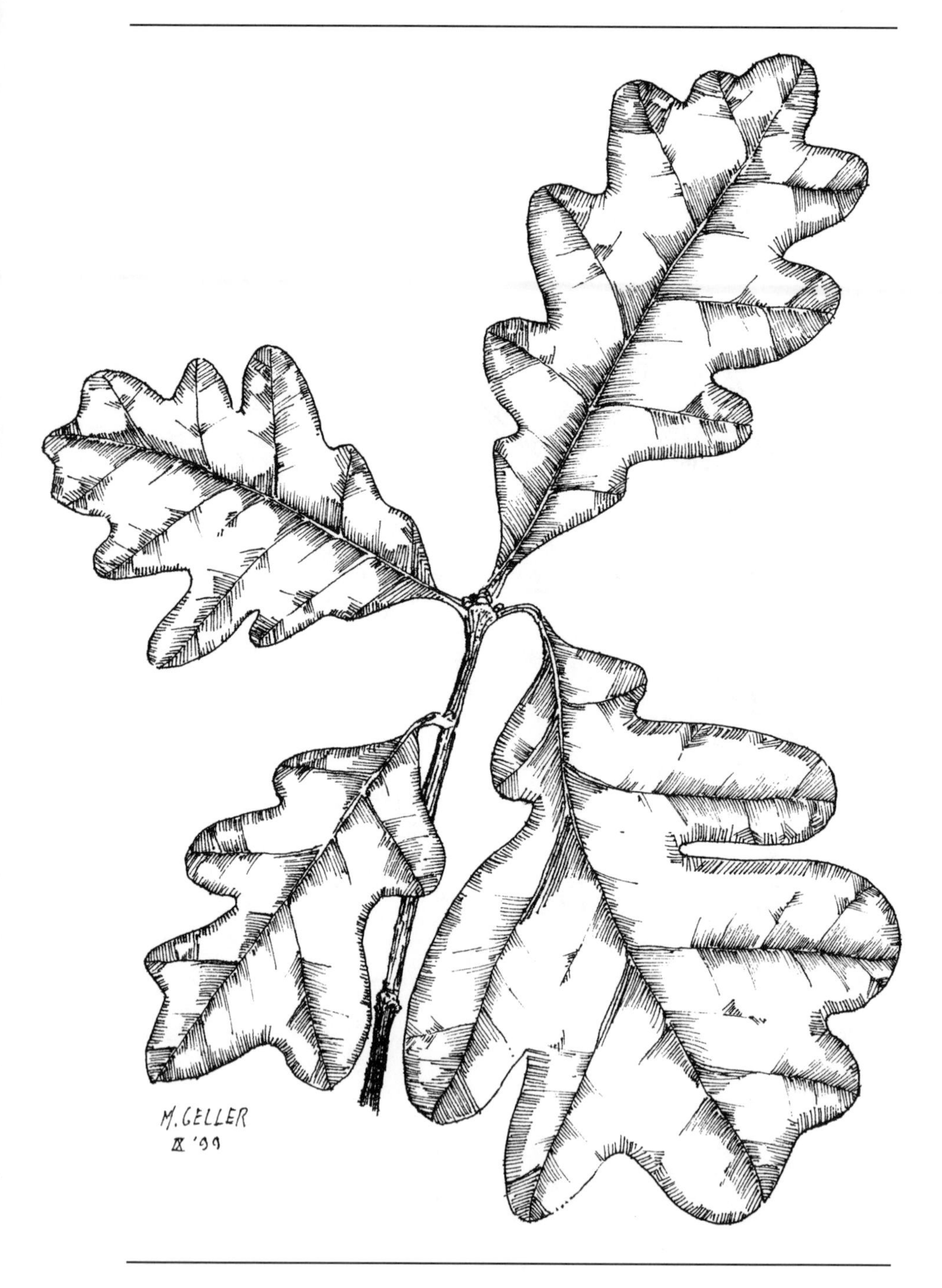

Figure 14. *Quercus alba,* white oak. The lobes of these leaves are arranged in rows. Figure 7 shows the lobes of the red maple, which are arranged in a palmate pattern.

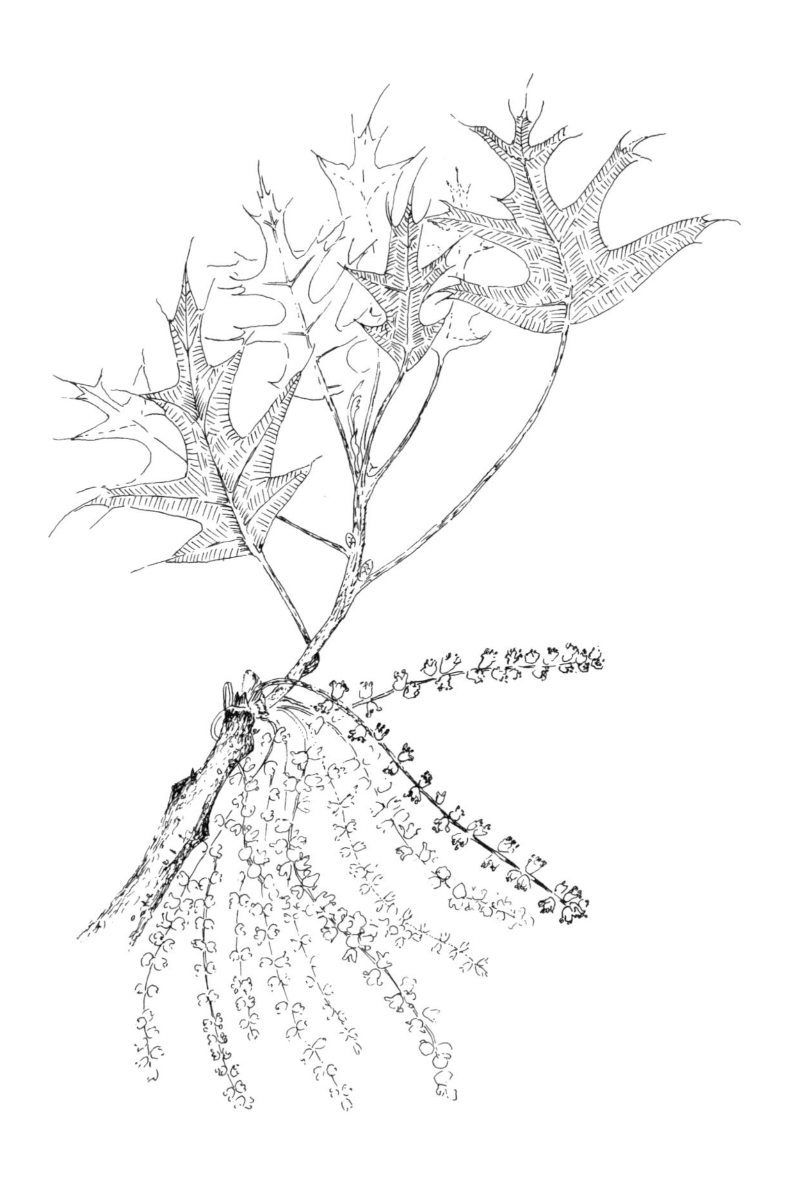

Figure 15. *Quercus coccinea,* scarlet oak, leaf and flowers. Many oaks have lobed leaves, which may or may not have "bristle tips." The scarlet oak shows this feature, but the white oak (Fig. 14) does not. The bristle tip is a vein that extends past the leaf blade and is a useful diagnostic characteristic for oaks. Some oaks have nonlobed leaves with bristle tips along their edges, while other species lack this feature. The illustration also shows this plant's wind-pollinated flowers, which lack showy petals found in flowers whose pollen is transferred by animals.

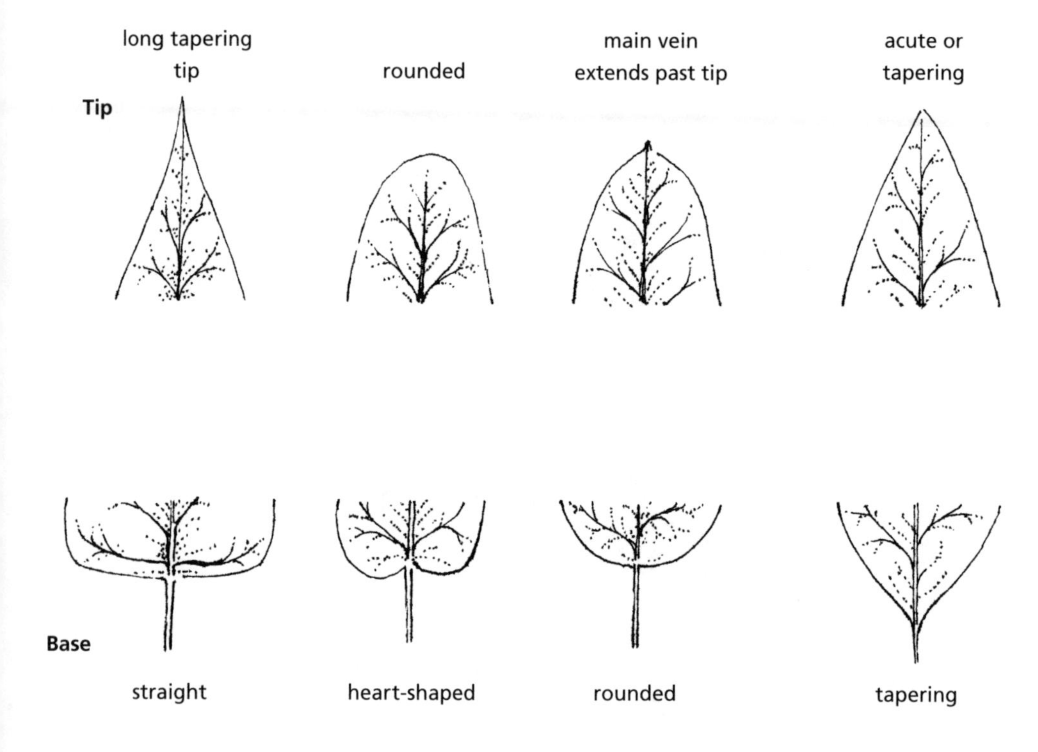

Figure 16. Shapes of the tips and bases of leaves. All of the leaf bases illustrated above are regular. That is, one side pretty much mirrors the other side. A few plants have irregular, or asymmetrical, leaf bases, in which case they have one type of base on one side and another type of base on the opposite side. For example, an asymmetrical leaf might have a tapered leaf base on one side while the opposite side has a rounded leaf base. Plants are very variable in the shapes of the tips and bases of their leaves, and depending on the species, any base might be found with any tip.

Figure 17. *Magnolia virginiana,* magnolia, a plant with leaves that have a smooth margin. This species shows an entire leaf (one with a smooth margin). This species has another distinctive feature. The base of the leaf stem forms a stipule scar that extends around the twig or branch, forming a ringlike line.

Figure 18. Another view of *Magnolia virginiana,* showing the flower and the ring-like stipule scar.

Figure 19. *Kalmia latifolia,* mountain laurel, leaves and flowers. This species also has leaves with a smooth margin.

Figure 20. *Lyonia mariana,* staggerbush. Another plant that has a leaf with a smooth margin (also called "entire").

Figure 21. *Amelanchier spp.,* Juneberry, showing a leaf with fine teeth. The leaves of this plant sometimes have a rounded, slightly heart-shaped base. Note that right below the lowest bud, you can see where the twig and the branchlet are separated. The latter is darker colored. In this species and a few other species, a series of rings marks the point where this year's growth (the twig) begins and the previous year's growth (the branchlet) left off.

Figure 22. *Prunus serotina,* black cherry. These leaves have fine teeth. On cherry leaves, the lowest tooth is often modified into dark-colored glands. Unfortunately, this characteristic feature is easy to miss.

Figure 23. *Castanea dentata* and *C. pumila,* Eastern chinquapin and American chestnut. This illustrates two plants with similar leaves and buds, both having coarse teeth and false end buds. The leaves of the chestnut are considerably larger, about twice the size of the chinquapin's. American chestnut trees were once abundant, but have been all but exterminated by a fungus that attacks saplings. Fortunately, the plant can sprout from a stump, and a few individuals survive to reach a height of about 30 feet before being stricken.

Figure 24. *Gaultheria procumbens,* false wintergreen. This small plant (usually under 3 inches) has leaves with few, coarse teeth and a distinctive whitish streak down the center. Note also the woody capsule.

Figure 25. *Comptonia peregrina,* sweet fern. This plant has a leaf that can be described as either coarsely toothed or lobed. The winter twig is also illustrated.

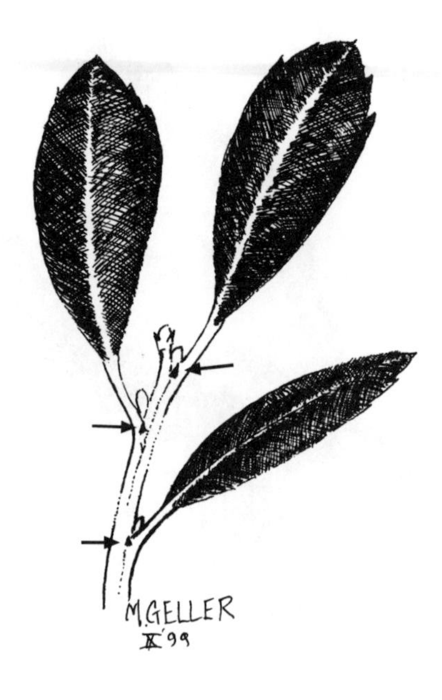

Figure 26. *Ilex glabra,* inkberry. This species as well as bayberry and a few others have leaves that are mostly smooth-edged but with a few teeth toward the tip. One important feature of the genus *Ilex* is the small triangular, black stipules or stipule scars (arrows; see also Figs. 31 and 33). Magnified about two times (2x).

Figure 27. *Myrica pensylvanica* and *M. cerifera,* bayberry and wax myrtle. These species are similar, with leaves that are mostly smooth-edged but with a few teeth toward the tip. Leaves and twigs are fragrant when crushed, and covered with yellow resin dots that look like small droplets of yellow liquid when seen in the right light (use hand lens). Magnified about two times (2x).

Figure 28. *Betula populifolia,* gray birch. This plant has leaves with double teeth, that is, the few coarse teeth have many fine teeth on them. Note also the leave's long tapering tip. Like other wind-pollinated plants (e.g., the oaks in Fig. 15 and the red maple in Fig. 7), the flowers of this plant are reduced and lack showy petals.

Figure 29. *Ulmus* Americana and *U. rubra,* American elm and slippery elm. Both species are rare in this area. Both have leaves with double teeth. The buds of the latter species have hairy scales.

Figure 30. Leaves of common species of *Rhododendron.* The edges of these leaves look finely toothed at first examination. Actually, they have smooth edges but are lined with tiny hairs, or *cilia.* Upper illustration of edge greatly magnified. Leaf magnified about two times (2x).

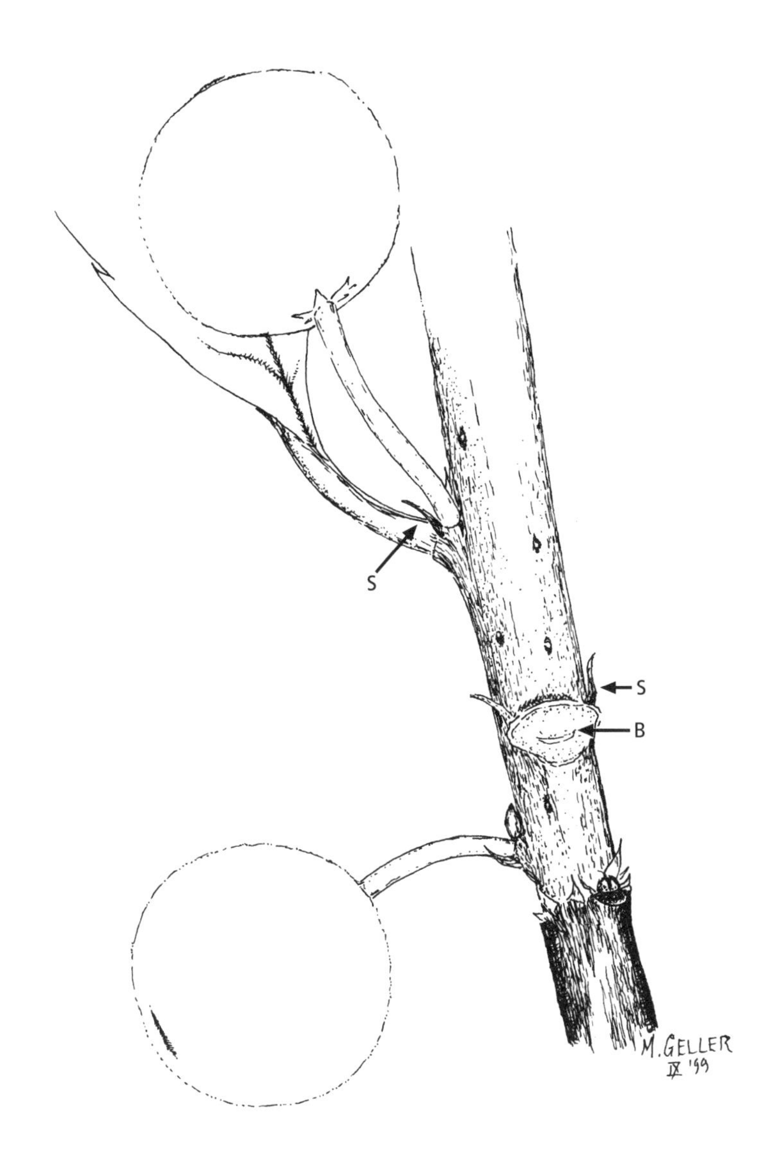

Figure 31. *Ilex laevigata,* smooth winterberry, magnified about 10x. Note the dark, triangular stipules (S) and the leaf scar with one bundle scar (B). Fleshy red berries help you identify this plant, which is typically found in wet areas. Compare smooth winterberry to the black cherry in Figure 6, which shows a plant with three bundle scars.

Figure 32. *Smilax rotundifolia,* greenbrier. This vine forms dense tangles, in part by grasping branches of other plants with tendrils, which in this case are modified stipules that are typically paired. Other vines climb upwards, using tendrils to wrap around and grasp other plants.

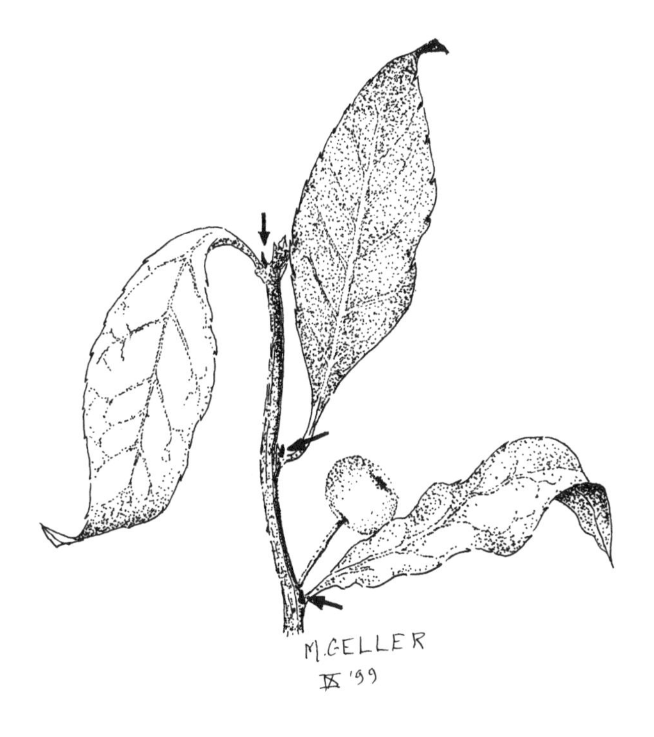

Figure 33. Another view of smooth winterberry. This shows both stipules (arrows) and leaves on the twigs of this species.

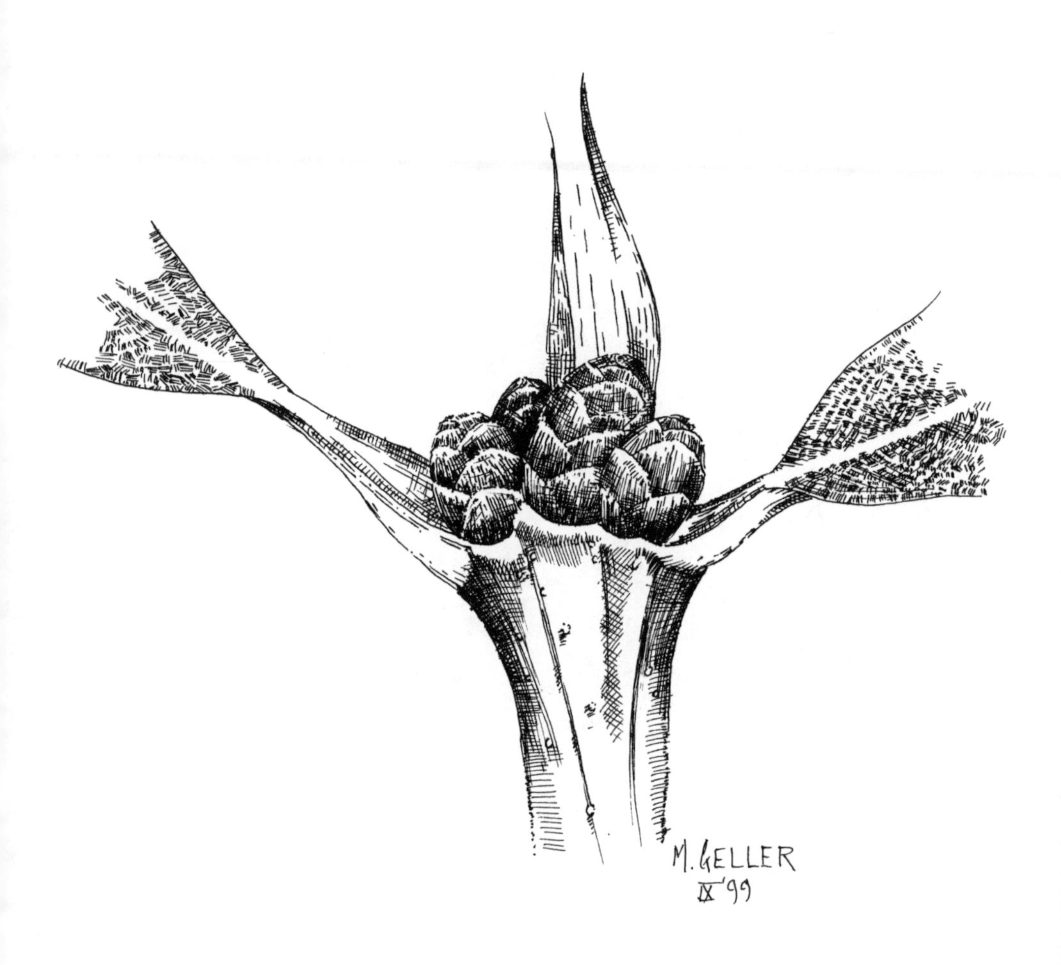

Figure 34. Clustered end buds of *Quercus spp.,* the oaks. The tip of an oak magnified about 40x. Oaks and azaleas have this distinctive feature, although the latter have one very large bud surrounded by several of a much smaller size (Fig. 35).

Figure 35. Clustered end buds of *Rhododendron spp.,* the azaleas. Azaleas have one large flower bud, usually with much smaller leaf buds around it. Magnified about two times (2x).

Figure 36. *Salix nigra,* black willow, twig. Willows have a single bud scale that covers the bud, much like a cap. This gives the bud a smooth, unbroken appearance.

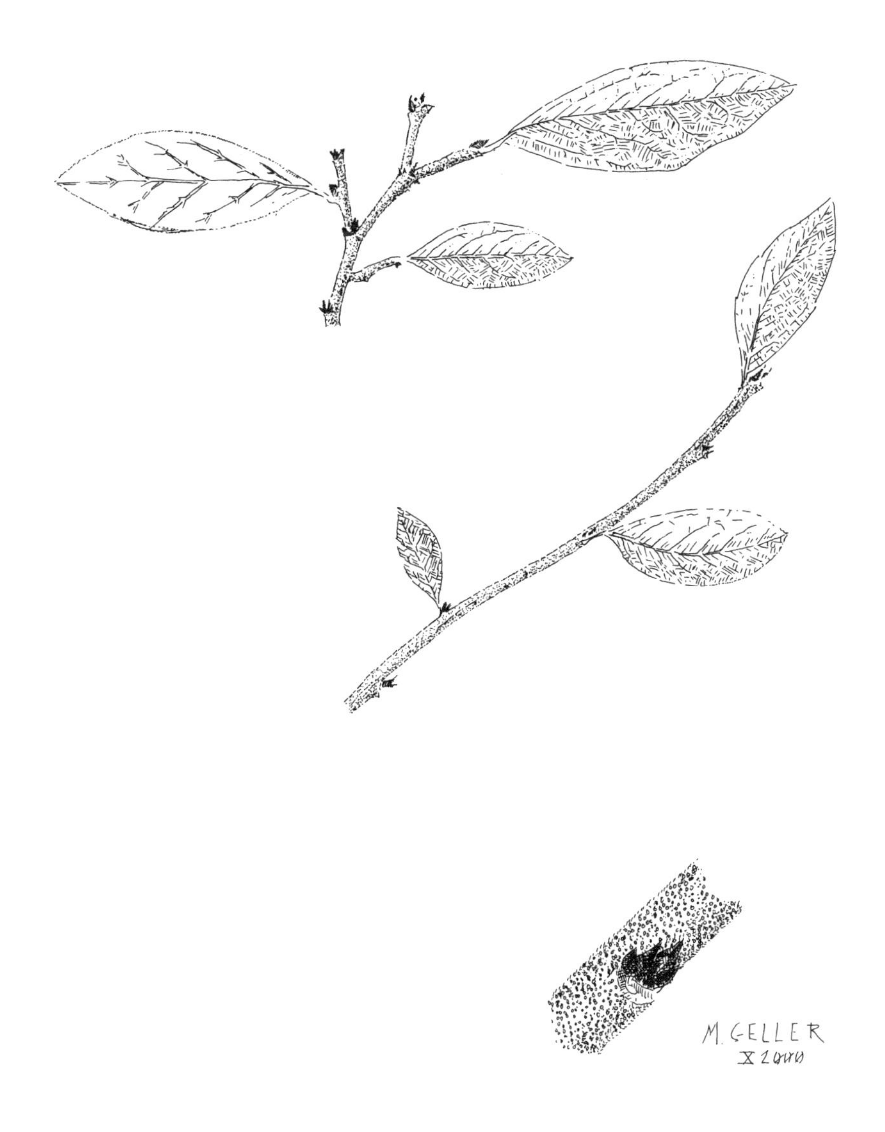

Figure 37. Leaves, twigs, and buds of *Vaccinium spp.,* blueberries. The lower illustration shows a close-up of the lateral bud of this plant. While the buds are small, you can see how the bud scales are arranged in the enlarged view of the leaf scar. In this and in virtually all other plants, the bud scales do not emerge directly above the leaf scar but arise from the sides. Blueberries are distinctive in that the twigs and branches are covered with a multitude of tiny white dots that look like very small speckles (or pimples).

Figure 38. Distinctive pattern of bud scales in *Populus spp.,* poplars. The lowest bud scales usually face the sides of the bud as you look directly at the bud with the leaf scar facing you. These bud scales clasp the sides of the bud. In poplars, on the other hand, the first bud scale is centrally located above the leaf scar. Compare this illustration to Figures 6 and 37, which show the more typical pattern.

Figure 39. Flower bud of *Viburnum nudum,* wild raisin. Two features of this plant are noteworthy. First, the flower bud looks like a bird's head with two large scales and a portion of a smaller one often visible between the two. Second, the lateral buds have two scales that join in the center, much like two halves of a clamshell. These also lie flat against the twig.

Figure 40. End buds of *Cornus florida,* flowering dogwood. There are two types of end bud on this plant. Leaf buds look very much like lateral buds. However, flower buds (lower illustration) are larger, much rounder, and stalked.

Figure 41. *Leucothoe racemosa,* swamp sweetbells. This illustrates the long, spike-like cluster of flower buds that is a distinctive feature of this species. These reddish-colored spikes are often present over winter along with a similarly shaped cluster of woody capsules. Sometimes clusters of flower buds and open and closed capsules can be found on the same plant. Leatherleaf (*Chamaedaphne calyculata*), a short shrub often found growing together with swamp sweetbells along ponds and streams, has a similar feature.

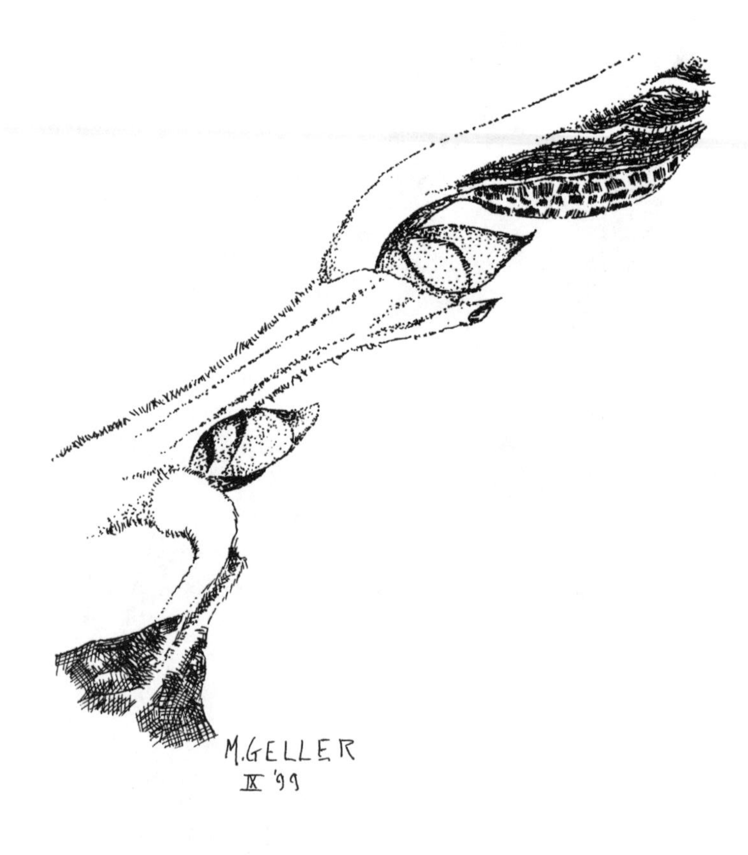

Figure 42. A false end, or false terminal, bud. Huckleberries (*Gaylussacia spp.*), blueberries (*Vaccinium*), and other plants have this feature. Note the small, dead stem to one side of the end bud and the angled position of the bud. These features help identify the false end bud. Magnified about ten times (10x). Figures 23 and 37 also show plants with false end buds.

Figure 43. *Clethra alnifolia,* sweet pepperbush, showing a true end bud. In this plant, the end bud is much larger than the lateral buds. Magnified about three times (3x).

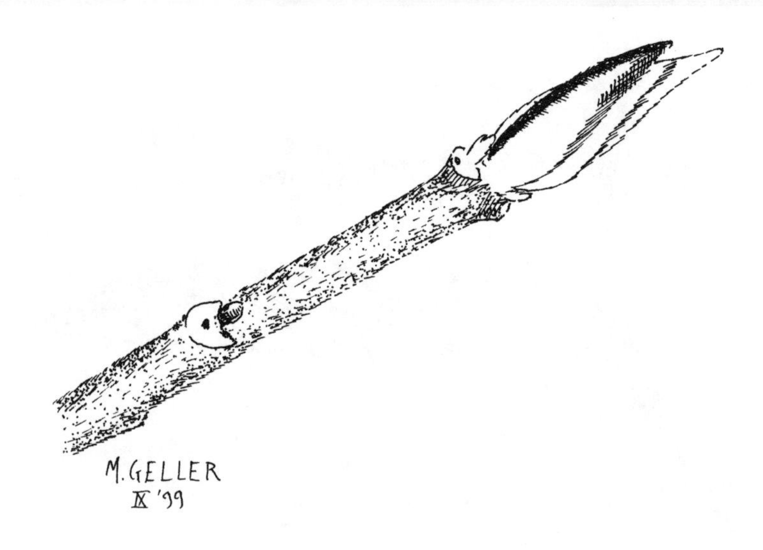

Figure 44. A true end bud of sweet pepperbush magnified 10x.

Figure 45. Capsules of *Leucothoe racemosa,* swamp sweetbells. A branch and twig with unripe capsules on the left can be compared to ripe open capsules (*center*). The illustration on the right shows a magnified view of the hard, woody capsule. Note how the flower buds (Fig. 41) have the same growth form as the capsules.

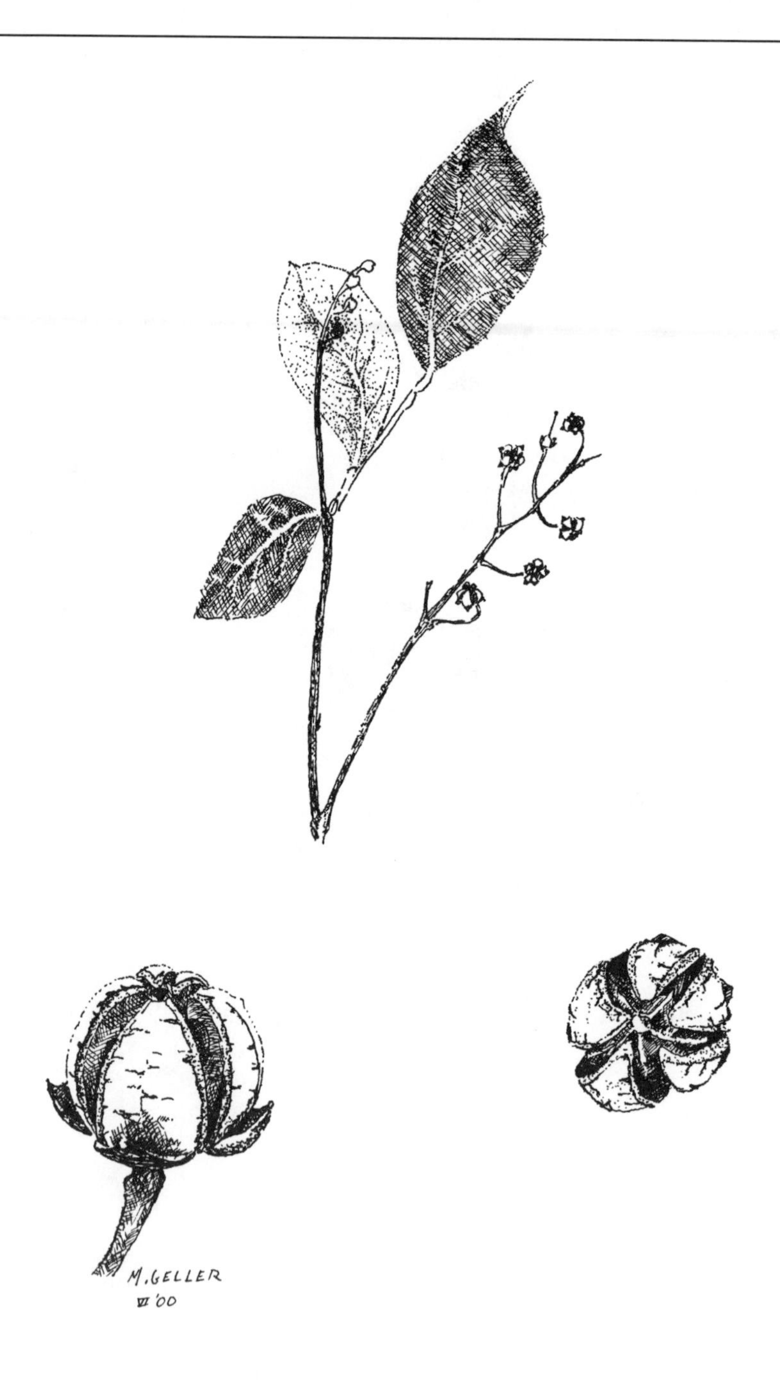

Figure 46. Capsules of *Lyonia ligustrina,* maleberry. A spikelike cluster of capsules (*upper view*) can be compared to two views of the hard, woody capsule (*lower*).

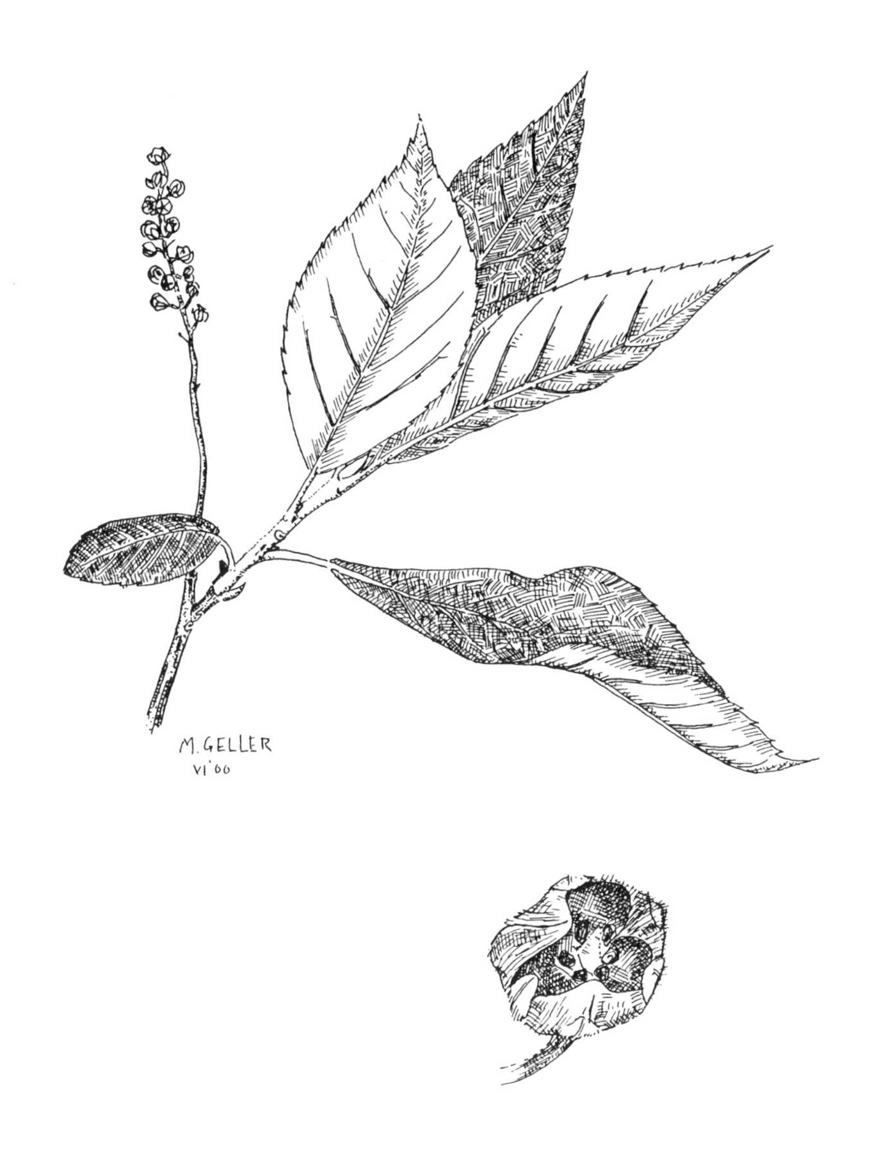

Figure 47. Capsules of *Clethra alnifolia,* sweet pepperbush. Unlike those of the previous two plants, the capsules of sweet pepperbush are delicate and easily crushed. They look like little peppercorns, and their elongate clusters typically persist almost year-round in this common plant. The lower illustration is a single capsule magnified about 10x.

Figure 48. Twig (*center*) and capsules of *Lyonia mariana,* staggerbush. A young, unopened capsule is shown in the upper drawing, while the lower illustration shows a cluster of older capsules. The immature capsules are green but become woody and mostly brown with a lighter tip and light stripes, or strips, that run from near the base to the tip of the capsule. In this species, the capsule is distinctly urn-shaped. The twig has reddish buds, a false end bud, and a smooth-edged leaf that often shows a little dimple at the tip where the leaf vein extends past the leaf edge.

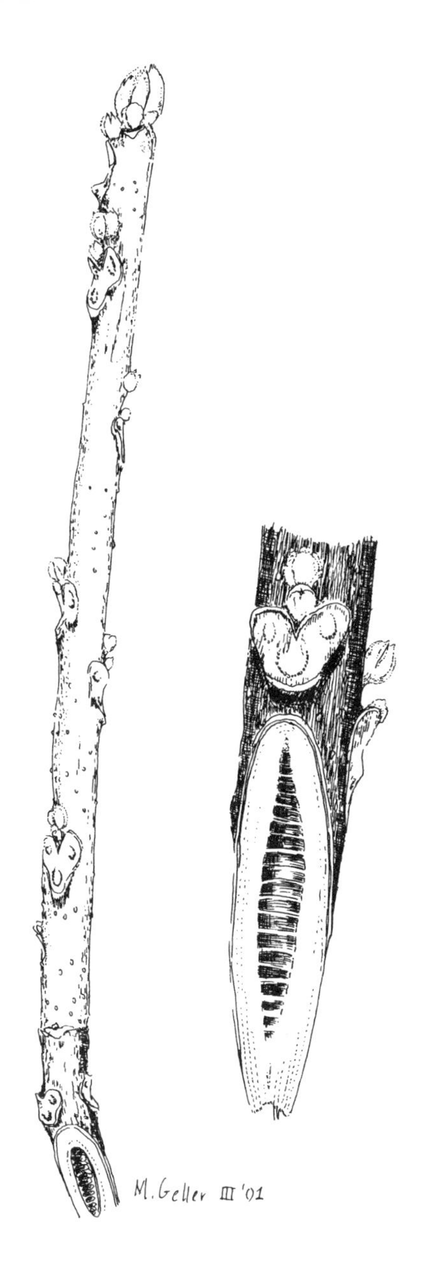

Figure 49. Chambered pith of *Juglans nigra,* black walnut. Several features besides the chambered pith are distinctive in this species. The leaf scars are large and lobed. In addition, the bundle scars are many, and they form three crescent-shaped lines. Several lateral buds can grow in a line above the leaf scar.

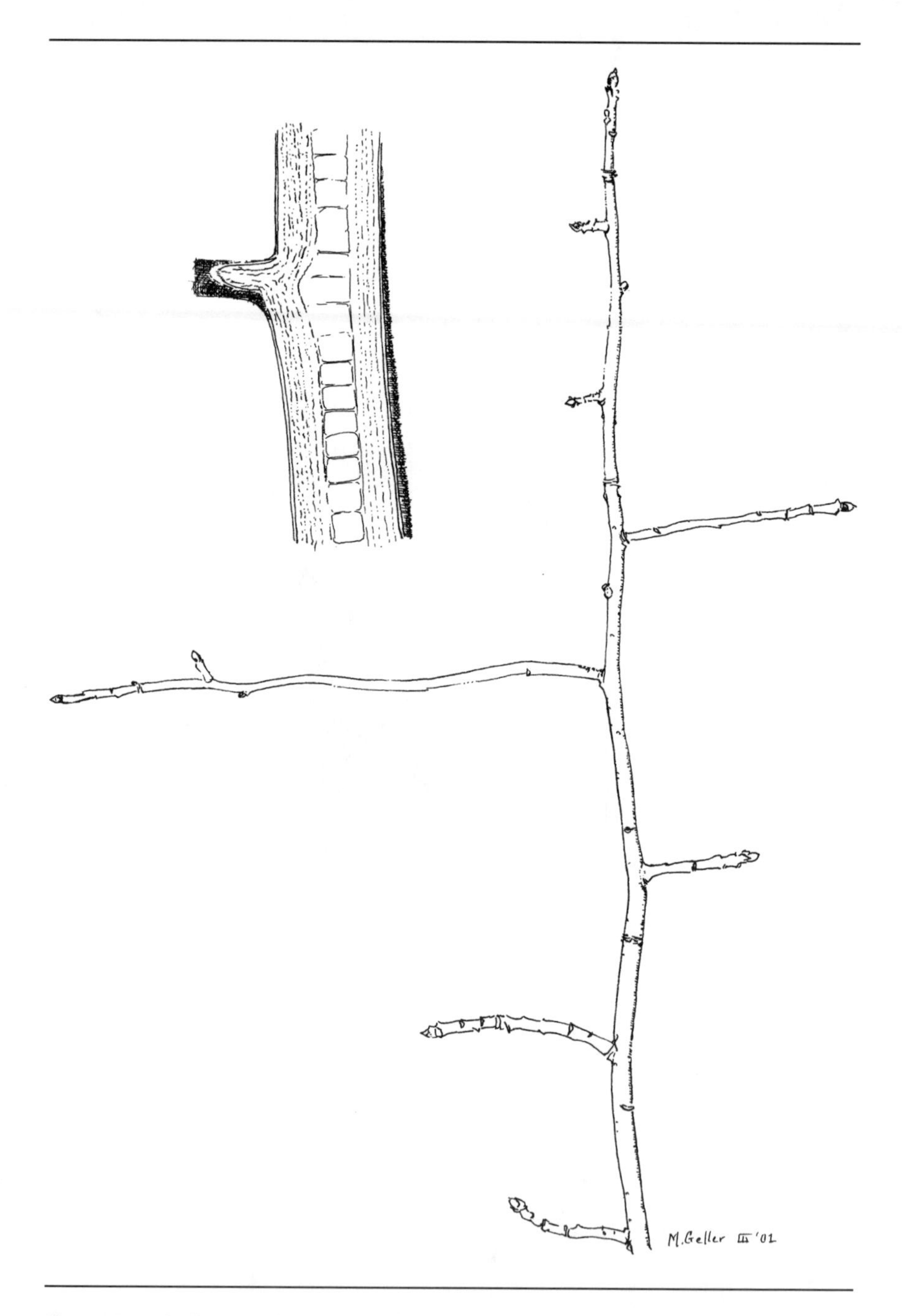

Figure 50. Diaphragmed pith in *Nyssa sylvatica,* black gum. The white pith in this species is broken up by transverse, woody membranes, or diaphragms. Note also the distinctive growth pattern of the twigs. Short spur branches emerge at almost right angles from the branch. The lines separating the twigs from the branchlets can also be seen.

Figure 51. Flower cluster and leaves of *Viburnum prunifolium,* smooth blackhaw.

Figure 52. Flower and leaves of *Cornus florida,* flowering dogwood.

Figure 53. Flowers of *Vaccinium corymbosum,* highbush blueberry (5x).

Figure 54. Flowers and leaves of *Gaylussacia spp.,* huckleberries.

Figure 55. Flower cluster of *Sassafras albidum.*

Figure 56. Flower buds of *Chamaedaphne calyculata,* leatherleaf (5x).

Figure 57. Flower cluster and leaves of *Lyonia mariana,* staggerbush (5x).

Figure 58. Flower cluster of *Prunus serotina,* black cherry.

Figure 59. Leaves and flowers of *Aronia spp.* Note the dark glands along the main vein on the upper surface of these leaves. Magnified about three times (3x).

Figure 60. Leaves and flower clusters of *Leucothoe racemosa,* swamp sweetbells (3x).

Figure 61. Flower cluster of *Clethra alnifolia,* sweet pepperbush.

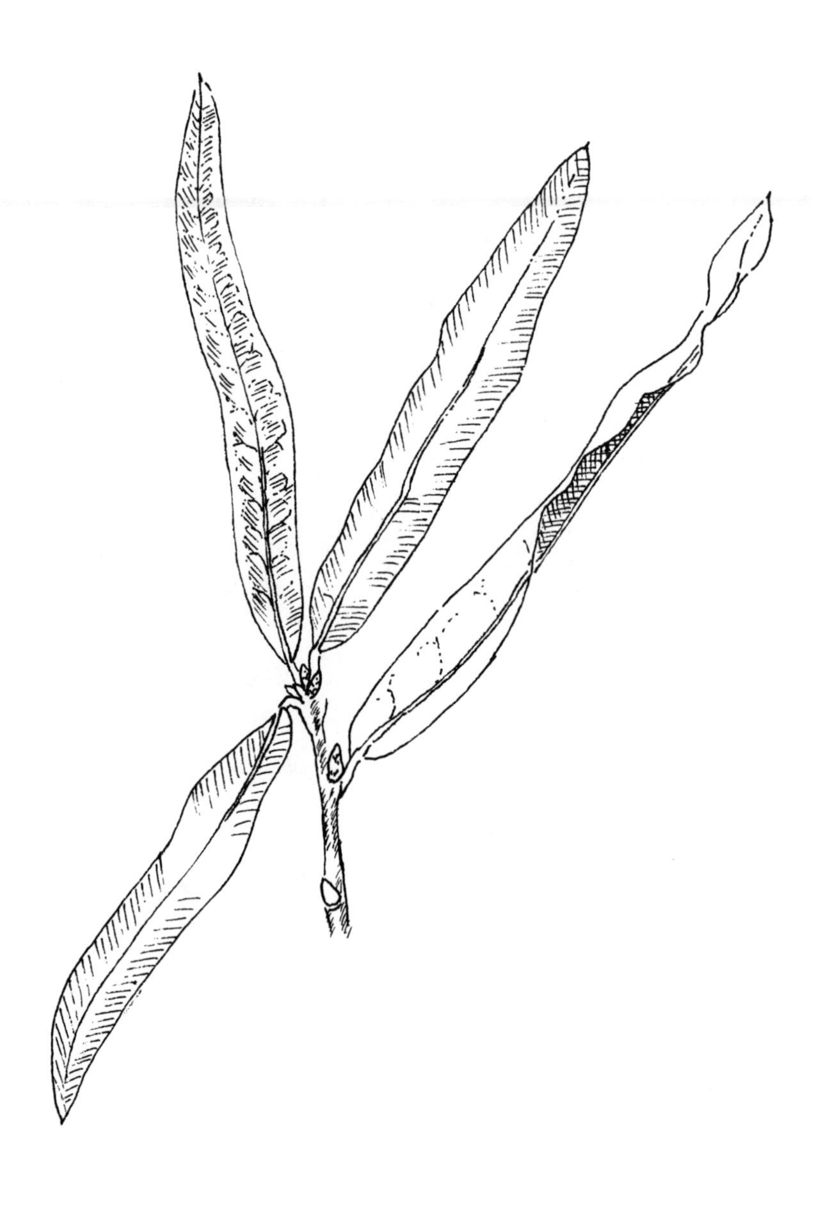

Figure 62. Leaves of *Quercus phellos,* willow oak.

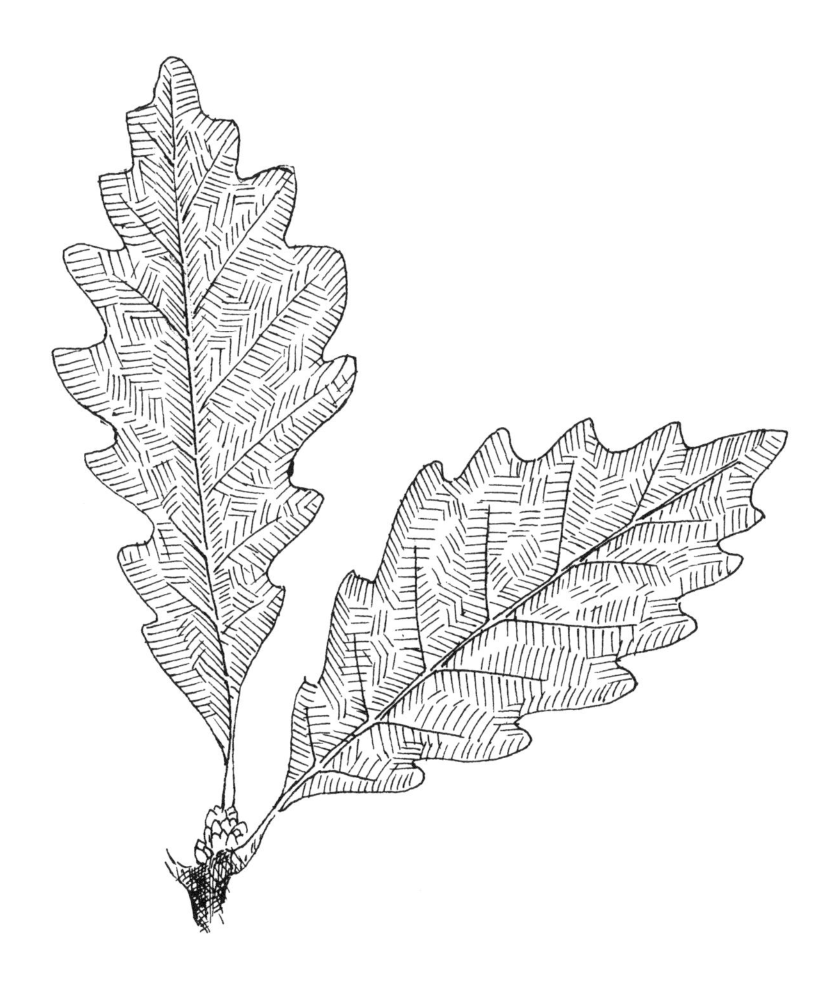

Figure 63. Leaves of *Quercus prinoides,* dwarf chestnut oak. The leaves of *Q. prinus,* chestnut oak, are larger, with edges that are more wavy and less deeply toothed.

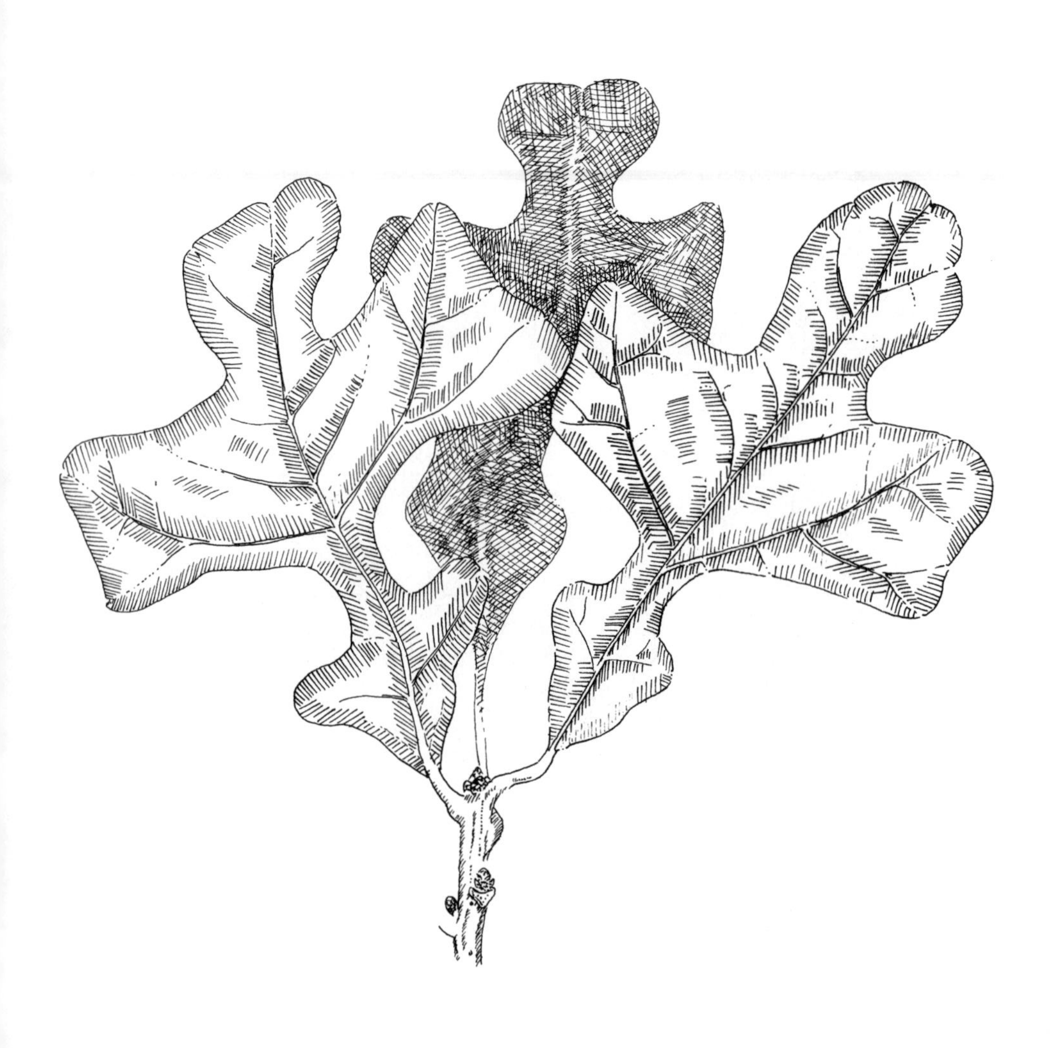

Figure 64. Leaves of *Quercus stellata,* post oak.

Figure 65. Leaves of *Quercus ilicifolia,* scrub oak.

Figure 66. Leaves of *Quercus falcata,* Spanish oak.

Chapter 10

Ethnobotany of the New Jersey Pine Barrens

Sandra Hartzog Bierbrauer

Ethnobotany is the study of various human cultures and how they identify and use plants over time. Plants have a multitude of uses: as food, fuel, and fiber; as raw materials for construction; as medicines; and as ornament. Plant communities provide habitat and food for the game species humans hunt for food, furs, and raw materials such as bone and antler.

In uncovering the diverse uses of the Pine Barrens species presented in this volume, I consulted Daniel Moerman's encyclopedic *Native American Ethnobotany* as well as works by Erichsen-Brown, Regensburg, and Tantaquidgeon for information on the Lenape Indians. Jack Cresson has given me very useful insights from his research in prehistoric archaeology. Historic information comes from Peter Wacker's chapter in Forman's 1979 classic, *Pine Barrens: Ecosystem and Landscape,* and from conversations with historian June Sheridan of the Atlantic County Historical Society and historic archaeologist Budd Wilson of Green Bank, New Jersey. Mention of Pine Barrens species' ornamental value is based on the work of Joe Arsenault, founder of Arrowwood Nursery. Medicinal uses of our woody flora comes from Moerman, cited above; from Herrick's study of the Iroquois; and Cecil Still's work on medicinal plants of New Jersey. A precaution is in order. Many medicinal uses cited in Table 10.2 are based on folk use, and have not been scientifically tested or verified. However, we must review the succession of people who lived in or traveled through the Pine Barrens to use its woody plants, before discussing their various uses over time.

People of the Pine Barrens

The cultural history of the New Jersey Pine Barrens began with the Paleo-Indians of the late Pleistocene, who were active here around 15,000 to 10,000 years ago. At this time, glaciers had retreated northward from their southernmost point in New Jersey, just north of the Pine Barrens today. Southern New Jersey had a strikingly different environment (Hartzog

1981). The vegetation was tundra and taiga, plant communities today found in northern Canada and Alaska. Tundra is open ground with lichens, sedges, grasses, and dwarf shrubs. Taiga has patches of spruce and fir forest and sphagnum bogs between the open tundra, and is found in slightly warmer areas. These two plant communities provided habitat for large ice-age mammals, including species now extinct, like mammoths and mastodons.

The Paleo-Indians hunted these ice-age mastodons, musk ox, and caribou using spears tipped with distinctive flint "Clovis" points and points made of caribou antler tips. These and other Paleo-Indian tools have been found by the hundreds across southern and coastal New Jersey. With the onset of the Holocene geological time period around 10,000 years ago, the climate warmed, dense forests of oak and pine returned, and the ice-age fauna vanished. However, Native Americans stayed and adapted to their changing environment, using forest and marine resources.

From about 10,000 years ago to the time of European contact, A.D. 1500–1600, a series of native cultures have been unearthed and identified by their changing styles of stone tools and their addition of new technology, such as bows and arrows, soapstone and ceramic containers, and smoking pipes. These tribes were hunter-gatherers, dining on seeds, nuts, berries, venison, bear, muskrat, snapping turtle, and various freshwater and marine finfish, crustaceans, and mollusks, like clams, oysters, and whelk. The Lenape, or Delaware, was the dominant tribe in New Jersey in A.D. 1600 and probably lived here for at least the previous several hundred years. As the Lenape culture is fairly well known, their uses of Pine Barrens plants will be discussed in detail.

History came to the Pine Barrens in the sixteenth century with Portuguese, Dutch, and Swedish explorers and fishermen. Dutch and Swedish settlers put down roots in coastal southern New Jersey in the seventeenth century. European expansion into the interior Pine Barrens was probably nil until the English East and West Jersey Proprietorships developed commercial ventures in the late seventeenth and eighteenth centuries. (The hereditary West Jersey Proprietorship still exists and owns some limited acreage within the Pine Barrens, according to my colleague and Proprietor, Nancy Haines Burke.) The Lenape were decimated by diseases the Europeans introduced during the seventeenth century. Although a handful of Lenape struggled in the Indian Mills reservation from 1758 to 1801, most migrated to Oklahoma or to Ontario, Canada. Some Lenape, such as the Goulds of Cumberland County and the Revey family of Monmouth County, became Europeanized members of the local population.

From 1670 on, under British rule, diverse immigrants came to southern New Jersey and began to utilize the Pine Barrens' resources. Early English and Irish surnames included Somers, Leeds, Hand, Buzby, Haines, and Richards; Swedish names included Mullica and Steelman (formerly Stahlmann); and Dutch names included Ong, of Ong's Hat, Conover (formerly Kouwenhoven), and Frambes (formerly Frambius). The French settler D'Estaile founded Estell Manor. Joseph Bonaparte settled on the western edge of the Pine Barrens and introduced white mulberry, *Morus alba,* in a failed attempt to establish a silk worm plantation. A distinguished French visitor was John Jacob Audubon, who spent three years up the Great Egg Harbor River in the early nineteenth century, documenting our native plants and animals. African-Americans, including both free and escaped slaves, found homes in "the Pines" before and during the Civil War in towns such as Mizpah and McKee City, Atlantic County. A noted member of this group was Dr. George Still, the "black doctor of the Pines." His great-grandnephew, Rutgers University biochemist Cecil Still, has compiled Dr. Still's work in a recent book (Still 1998). By the later nineteenth century, the list of immigrants included Italians, Ukrainians, Germans, Russians, and Ashkenazic Jews. The twentieth century brought displaced Japanese, Mexicans, and other Hispanics who came as migrant farm workers and settled. Other "Pineys" were ex-Philadelphians seeking a rural lifestyle. In short, the Pine Barrens, while sparsely settled, have been rich in cultural diversity (Wacker 1979; J. Sheridan, personal communication, 1999).

Utility

Trees, shrubs and vines, the "woody plants," have a number of obvious uses and some less obvious ones. Uses may change over time if better alternatives become available or if new uses are discovered. For all residents of the Pine Barrens, timber was a primary forest resource. Pine, oak, chestnut, hickory, and white cedar were, and still are, cut for construction lumber, boat building, fences, furniture, tools, and tool handles. The wood of smaller trees like red cedar, which does not easily rot, is used for fence posts and for moth-repellant storage chests. Persimmon was used for the heads of golf clubs, and is still used for furniture veneers. Ironwood,

Carpinus, was used by nineteenth-century shipbuilders for pulleys, and by early-twentieth-century submarine architects for engine bearings. White oak strips and woody vines were used for basketry, and finally bark strips of white cedar and a few other trees were used for fiber and cordage.

Fuel uses include hardwoods—oaks, red maple, and hickory—for firewood. Hickory wood in particular was used in prehistoric times, by early colonists, and is still preferred today for smoking fish and meats. Pitch pine was and is still a preferred species to make charcoal, which burns hotter and more cleanly than unprocessed softwoods (conifers). Charcoal was the primary fuel used by late-eighteenth- and early-nineteenth-century industries in mid-Atlantic states, as well as the fuel preferred in urban residential fireplaces.

Food

Many Pine Barrens trees and shrubs provide food for humans directly as roots, nuts, and berries, or indirectly as mast (nuts and seeds) and foliage to feed wildlife. Among the edible nuts are acorns from the oak subgenus *Leucobalanus,* which includes white, chestnut, post, and a few other oak species. White oak acorns were a staple starch while hickory nuts, rich in oils and protein, were an essential staple food for the prehistoric Native Americans. The American chestnut, a staple preferred by both Lenape and Europeans, was prevalent in our area before the early-twentieth-century blight. Some chestnuts still survive locally from stump sprouts. Black walnuts and butternuts were less common, but provided both a staple starch and interesting flavor.

The area is rich in edible fruits. Persimmon fruit, blueberries, huckleberries, grapes, and cranberries are used fresh, in preserves, and in wine. Other fruits include rose hips, blackberries, teaberries, sassafras, and beach plums, the latter found on the coastal shorelines. Some less tasty, but still nutritious, fruits include black cherries, chokeberries, and serviceberries. Hackberries were a starvation food. Sumac fruits make a pleasant "lemonade-like" beverage. Sassafras leaves are used as flavoring, especially in Creole cuisine as Filé powder. Sassafras roots make a pleasant tea, while red maple sap can be cooked down to make a tasty, sweet syrup. Many other edible Pine Barrens plants are herbaceous, such as *Peltandra,* or tuckahoe, which produces an edible starchy tuber, and thus is not in the purview of this book.

Medicines

Pine Barrens plants have had medicinal uses from prehistoric times through the nineteenth century and have been used to treat a wide variety of maladies. The 1895 *United States Pharmacopoeia* includes many such plants with recipes for preparing and compounding drugs from them. Around 1900, the *U.S. Pharmacopoeia* and the pharmaceutical industry increasingly turned to refined plant products, such as aspirin from salicylic acid, or to completely synthetic products. However, a few of our native species, such as wintergreen, are still included.

Aspirin, as mentioned above, was probably the most widely used "wonder drug" of the late nineteenth and twentieth centuries, and of course is still used today. Aspirin—acetyl-salicylic acid—is derived from salicylic acid, present in several different plants, such as willow bark, *Salix spp.;* the garden flower meadowsweet, *Filipendula;* and our local wintergreen, *Gaultheria.* Aspirin's traditional uses include reducing fever and treating painful headaches and inflammation. It is an effective anticoagulant, prescribed at higher doses to treat heart attacks caused by blood clots and at lower doses to prevent heart disease and strokes. Wintergreen oil is used in liniment, and salicylic acid is used in facial scrub preparations for control of acne. Aspirin is also used to control autoimmune diseases like lupus. While aspirin's undesirable side effects are real, it is far safer than alternative anti-inflammatory treatments such as steroids like prednisone.

Research on "nutriceuticals," that is, foods that also have therapeutic value, is active today. The cranberry is a prime example. Traditional "folk" medicine used cranberry juice as an effective treatment for urinary tract infections, which often respond poorly to antibiotic treatment. Flavonoid compounds in cranberries, as well as the vitamin C present in this fruit, have been identified and documented as effective for this problem. Another botanical folk remedy is the use of bilberry extract for vision problems and damage to the retina. Bilberries, *Vaccinium myrtillis,* are the European cousin of our blueberries. Our native lowbush and highbush blueberries, as well as our native grapes, contain antioxidant anthocyanins, which help protect the retina. Antioxidant therapy, including carotenes and anthocyanins, has been recommended to help prevent or retard the "dry" form of macular degeneration.

Prehistoric Native Americans once used woody plant extracts to treat a wide variety of conditions, now treated with modern pharmaceutical

Table 10.1. Glossary of Medical Terms

Analgesic: pain reliever
Antibiotic: kills or inhibits growth of living organisms, largely bacteria
Antifungal: kills or inhibits growth of fungi
Antihelminthic: kills or eliminates intestinal worms
Anti-inflammatory: reduces redness, swelling, and pain
Antiseptic: inhibits bacteria
Antiviral: inhibits or kills viruses
Astringent: causes tissues to shrink
Carminative: reduces gas in the digestive tract
Cathartic: powerful laxative
Decoction: medicine prepared by boiling plant parts
Diuretic: stimulates urination
Emetic: stimulates vomiting
Infusion: medicine prepared by soaking plant parts in hot or cold water, as in "teas"
Tincture: extract of plant parts in alcohol
Vermifuge: controls intestinal worms

products. A complete review is beyond the scope of this work, but a short list of medical terms is presented in Table 10.1, followed by a list of medicinally useful plants in Table 10.2.

Modern medicine relies on antibiotics, some of which, like streptomycin, were derived from Pine Barrens microbes. Now, in the early twenty-first century, we have a new medical dilemma: microbes developing drug resistance faster than modern pharmaceutical companies can develop new drugs. We still have only a limited array of antiviral and antifungal products, and need to find safer and more effective drugs to fight cancer. Interest in natural plant products has been renewed by both pharmaceutical researchers and alternative health care providers. The classic example of a new drug derived from a tree is Taxol, from the Pacific yew. Taxol was discovered within the last decade and is now the drug of choice to fight breast and prostate cancers. Hopefully, woody Pine Barrens species will be sources of the next important new medicines.

Ornamentals

Through the late nineteenth and most of the twentieth century, local residents gathered Pine Barrens plants for the florist trade. Pine cones, grapevines, ground pine, or *Lycopodium spp.*, and Mt. Laurel foliage were

Table 10.2. Uses of Pinelands Woody Plants

Species	*Food Use*	*Medicinal Use*	*Raw Material Use*
Acer rubrum, red maple	Sap: sweetener; inner bark	Bark decoction: eyes, PMS	Wood: bowls, baskets, fuel
Alnus serrulata, speckled alder		Bark: analgesic, cathartic	Tinder to start fire
Amelanchier spp., serviceberry	Fruit: fresh, dried	Bark: antihelminthic, antidiarrheal, gyneco-logic	Ornamental flowering tree
Arctostaphylos uva-ursi, bearberry	Fruit: fresh, dried	Leaf, twig infusion: skin, kidneys, analgesic	
Baccharis halimifolia, groundsel tree		Bark: disinfectant, dermatologic, kidney	Tinder to start fire
Betula nigra, river birch		Leaf, bark infusion: dysentery, urinary tract	Wood: fuel
Betula populifolia, gray birch		Bark decoction: skin, hemorrhoids, cuts	Wood: fuel; young branches: decorative
Carya spp., hickories	Nuts: meat, oil, spice	Bark infusion: analgesic, multiuse	Wood: fuel, pestles, tool handles, arrows
Castanea dentata, chestnut	Nuts: staple, spice	Leaf decoction: cough, gastrointestinal	Bark: brown dye; wood for construction
Celastrus scandens, bittersweet		Root bark infusion: multiuse	Ornamental fruit
Celtis occidentalis, hackberry	Fruit: food, spice	Bark decoction: gynecological aid	Wood: fuel
Cephalanthus occidentalis, buttonbush		Leaf, bark infusion: eyewash, multiuse	
Chamaecyparis thyoides, Atlantic white cedar		Leaf decoction or steam: analgesic, headaches	Wood: decay-resistant, canoes, paddles, bowls, shingles, construc-tion; bark: fiber, rope, twine

(*continued*)

Table 10.2. *(continued)*

Species	*Food Use*	*Medicinal Use*	*Raw Material Use*
Chamaedaphne calyculata, leatherleaf	Beverage: leaf tea		
Chimaphila maculata, spotted false wintergreen		Roots: analgesic, antidiarrheal, colds, "ague"	
Clethra alnifolia, sweetpepper bush		Bark: gall bladder, antiemetic, febrifuge	Ornamental shrub, moist sites
Comptonia peregrina, "sweetfern"		Leaf infusion: skin poultice, poison ivy	Ornamental shrub, dry sites
Cornus florida, dogwood		Leaves: smoked; bark extract: multiuse	Wood: carving, tools, decoration, fuel; ornamental
Diospyros virginiana, persimmon	Fruit: jam, pies, wine	Bark, sap: liver, gastrointestinal, sore throat	Wood: fuel, tools
Epigaea repens, trailing arbutus, Mayflower		Leaf decoction: multiuse	Ornamental
Fraxinus pennsylvanicus, green ash	Inner bark: food	Bark: cathartic, emetic	Wood: tool handles, fuel
Gaultheria procumbens, wintergreen	Fruit: edible, flavor	Leaf extract: kidney, antirheumatic, febrifuge, dysentery, multiuse	
Gaylussacia baccata, tall huckleberry	Fruit: ceremonial food	Leaf and bark infusion, dysentery	
Gaylussacia frondosa, *G. dumosa*, huckleberries	Fruit: fresh, dried		
Gleditsia triacanthos, honey locust	Seed pulp: beverage	Bark: antihelminthic, dyspepsia, viral diseases	Wood: fuel
Hibiscus moscheutos, marsh mallow		Urinary aid	
Hudsonia tomentosa, beach heath		"Blood medicine"	

Table 10.2. (*continued*)

Species	*Food Use*	*Medicinal Use*	*Raw Material Use*
Hypericum spp., St. Johnswort		Multiuse	
Ilex opaca, American holly		Leaf, bark, fruit infusions: eye wash, gastrointestinal	Wood: spoons, decorative carving; foliage: ornamental
Ilex verticillata, winterberry holly		Bark decoction: physic	Ornamental landscape shrub
Juglans nigra, black walnut	Nuts: spice	Toxic: cathartic	Nut hulls: dye, insecticidal oil; wood: tool handles, gun stocks, furniture
Juniperus virginiana, Eastern red cedar	Berries: flavoring	Fruit: antihelminthic; leaves: antirheumatic, colds	Wood: decay-resistant, posts, moth-resistant storage chests
Kalmia angustifolia, dwarf laurel, sheepkill		Leaves: analgesic, toxic	
Kalmia latifolia, mountain laurel		Leaf infusion: liniment, analgesic, orthopedic	Ornamental landscape shrub
Leiophyllum buxifolium, sand myrtle	Fruit: spring beverage	"Spring tonic"	
Leucothoe racemosa, swamp sweetbells		Leaf infusion: rheumatism	Ornamental shrub
Ligustrum vulgare, privet		Toxic	Hedge species
Lindera benzoin, spice bush	Fruit, twigs: beverage, spice	Bark infusion: multiuse remedy	Ornamental shrub
Liquidambar styraciflua, sweet gum	Bark for tea	Bark, pitch: antidiarrheal, skin salve	Wood: fuel
Liriodendron tulipifera, tulip poplar		Bark infusion: antihelminthic, gastrointestinal	Wood: canoes, containers

(*continued*)

Table 10.2. *(continued)*

Species	*Food Use*	*Medicinal Use*	*Raw Material Use*
Lonicera spp., honeysuckle			Fiber: baskets; ornamental
Lyonia mariana, staggerbush		Bark infusion: dermatological aid	
Magnolia virginiana, sweetbay magnolia		Twig and leaf decoction: fevers, colds	Wood: fuel
Mitchella repens, partridge berry	Fruit: fresh, dried	Leaf, twig, root, fruit decoction: multiuse	
Morus rubra, red mulberry	Fruit: food, beverage	Roots: antihelminthic, cathartic	
Myrica pensylvanica, bayberry		Bark: "blood purifier," kidneys, emetic, vermifuge	Wax for candles, fragrance
Nyssa sylvatica, black gum	Fruit: dried	Bark infusion: emetic, antihelminthic, TB remedy	Wood: fuel, tool handles, mauls
Parthenocissus quinquefolia, Virginia creeper		Jaundice, antidiarrheal, urinary aid	Vine: fiber, baskets
Pinus echinata, shortleaf pine		Pitch pellets: analgesic, cathartic	Wood: fuel, dimensional lumber
Pinus rigida, pitch pine		Pitch: antirheumatic	Wood: fuel, carving, construction, charcoal; pitch; needles: insecticidal smoke; cones: ornamental
Pinus strobus, Eastern white pine	Young male catkins: food	Pitch: analgesic for skin	Wood: fuel, construction
Pinus virginiana, scrub or Virginia pine		Multiuse, antihelminthic	Wood: fuel
Platanus occidentalis, sycamore, plane tree		Bark decoction: antidiarrheal, gynecologic, throat, cold remedy	Wood: fuel

Table 10.2. (*continued*)

Species	*Food Use*	*Medicinal Use*	*Raw Material Use*
Populus deltoides, cottonwood poplar		Leaf, buds: antiscurvy; herbal steam: wounds, snakebite	Pulp wood
Populus tremuloides, quaking aspen		Antihelminthic, gastrointestinal	Pulp wood
Prunus americana, American plum	Fruit: food, beverage	Bark: cough medicine, kidney aid	Inner bark: dye; wood: fuel
Prunus serotina, black cherry	Fruit: food, beverage	Bark: cough, cold remedy; blood tonic, antidiarrheal	Wood: furniture
Pyrus (Aronia) arbutifolia, melanocarpa, chokeberries	Fruit: fresh, dried	Fruit: cold remedy	Ornamental shrub
Quercus alba, white oak	Nuts: staple starch	Bark infusion: multiuse	Wood: multiuse—fuel, tools, baskets
Quercus bicolor, swamp white oak	Nuts: staple starch	Bark: cholera, TB remedy	Bark: cleaning agent; wood: fuel
Quercus marylandica, blackjack oak	Nuts: starvation food	Bark infusion: analgesic	Wood: fuel
Quercus phellos, willow oak	Nuts: starvation food	Bark infusion: analgesic	Wood: fuel
Quercus prinus, chestnut oak	Nuts: staple starch		Wood: fuel; bark: dye
Quercus stellata, post oak	Nuts: staple starch	Bark infusion: anti-diarrheal, disinfectant	Wood: fuel, baskets, furniture
Quercus velutina, black oak	Nuts: starvation food	Bark infusion: cold remedy, multiuse	Bark: dye, tanning leather; wood: fuel, furniture
Rhus copallina, winged sumac	Fruit: beverage; ceremonial food	Bark: poultice for skin	Bark: dye; ornamental shrub
Rhus typhina, staghorn sumac	Fruit: beverage	Fruit: sore throat	Ornamental shrub

(*continued*)

Table 10.2. (*continued*)

Species	*Food Use*	*Medicinal Use*	*Raw Material Use*
Robinia pseudo-acacia, black locust	Leaf, bark: tea	Bark: emetic, analgesic	Wood: fences, dowels
Rosa spp., wild roses	Fruit: edible, tea	Fruit: cold remedy; bark and root: antihelminthic	
Rubus allegheniensis, blackberry	Fruit: fresh, dried	Canes: antidiarrheal	
Rubus flagellaris, dewberry	Fruit: fresh, dried, juice	Root: antidiarrheal	
Salix nigra, black willow		Bark infusion: analgesic, antidiarrheal, febrifuge	Twigs: basketry
Sambucus canadensis, elderberry	Fruit: wine, preserves	Bark: emetic, analgesic; fruit: rheumatism	
Sassafras albidum, sassafras	Root inner bark: tea; leaves: spice; fruit	Bark: antihelminthic, blood purifier, febrifuge, eye wash	Wood: furniture, incense
Smilax glauca, greenbriar	Root tubers	Twigs: analgesic	
Smilax laurifolia, laurel-leaf greenbriar	Root tubers, fried	Twig infusion: dermatological, burns	
Smilax rotundifolia, round-leaf greenbriar		Leaves: analgesic	
Tilia americana, basswood		Bark extract: gastrointestinal, diuretic	Wood: furniture, carving
Toxicodendron radicans, poison ivy		Poison, emetic, rheumatism	
Toxicodendron vernix, poison sumac		Febrifuge, urinary, respiratory aid	
Vaccinium angustifolium, swamp lowbush blueberry	Fruit: fresh, dried	Leaves: gastrointestinal aid; roots: blood purifier	
Vaccinium atrococcum, black highbush blueberry	Fruit: fresh, dried		

Table 10.2. *(continued)*

Species	*Food Use*	*Medicinal Use*	*Raw Material Use*
Vaccinium corymbosum, highbush blueberry	Fruit: fresh, dried	Roots: antispasmodic, gynecological aid	
Vaccinium macrocarpon, cranberry	Fruit: fresh, dried	Fruit: pleurisy, urinary tract	
Viburnum dentatum, arrowwood viburnum		Bark: contraceptive, poultice	Leaves: smoking
Viburnum lentago, nannyberry	Fruit: fresh, dried	Root extract: gynecological aid	
Vitis spp., grapes	Fruit: fresh, dried	Leaf infusion: gastro-intestinal, antidiarrheal, multiuse	Vines: basketry

collected to make into wreaths and chains for holiday décor. Trailing arbutus, *Epigea*, reached threatened status due to overharvesting for May Day bouquets in late Victorian times.

In the last twenty years, landscaping with native species has become a new Pine Barrens industry. The Pinelands Comprehensive Management Plan does mandate landscaping with native species in development under its jurisdiction. However, local residents are beginning to recognize the reason for this mandate, as native species are better suited to local soils and site conditions.

Our wetlands species include a number of attractive ornamentals now in cultivation—sweetbay magnolia, *M. virginiana;* swamp azalea, *Rhododendron viscosum;* and sweetpepper bush, *Clethra alnifolia*—that combine pretty flowers with delightul fragrances. Cultivars of our native evergreen holly, *Ilex opaca,* which have been grown and bred for years, are now joined by inkberry holly, *Ilex glabra,* and winterberry hollies, *Ilex verticillata* and *decidua.* For dry sites, mountain laurel, *Kalmia latifolia,* has attractive evergreen foliage, showy flowers, and an added advantage—it is not popular forage with deer. For extremely open, arid sites, bearberry, *Arctostaphylos uva-ursi,* is an excellent ground cover. "Pygmy" pines, the scrubby pitch pines of the east and west plains, are easily grown from seed and make interesting small landscape specimen trees. They are also excellent bonsai material.

Species of Special Merit

Many Pine Barrens species have multiple uses. For both commercial and ecological purposes, Atlantic white cedar, *Chamaecyparis thyoides,* is among the most valuable. Atlantic white cedar wood has a myriad of uses because it is resistant to decay, fine-grained, and easily carved, split, or sawn. It provides habitat for numerous threatened and endangered animal and plant species, and it is a good monitor of health or stress of freshwater wetlands. White oak is a multiuse hardwood tree, good for fuel, furniture and flooring, and wildlife habitat. It is a fire-resistant species, well adapted to Pine Barrens conditions. Our American chestnut was at one time a most valuable timber tree, as the wood is termite-resistant and has good tensile strength. Its nuts are small but very tasty, it makes an attractive shade tree, and it thrives in a range of soil types. Once common around the fringes of the Pine Barrens, it is slowly recovering from the early-twentieth-century blight. The genus *Vaccinium,* blueberries and cranberries, has been cultivated for its fruit, and merits further study for additional medicinal value. Our often under-appreciated pitch pine, *Pinus rigida,* is grown commercially as a timber tree in Appalachian Mountain states such as western North Carolina and West Virginia. Its ornamental value is certainly not sufficiently recognized.

Integrating Pine Barrens People and Their Plants

Clearly, woody plants were a major resource for prehistoric residents of, and travelers to, the Pine Barrens. We have direct archaeological evidence of wood used for wigwams and dugout canoes, other wooden objects preserved in peat bogs, and charred firewood, nuts, and seeds. Two local archaeologists, Richard Regensburg and Jack Cresson, have experimented with Pine Barrens woods, testing their uses as spear and arrow shafts, bows, handles, and billets (wooden hammers) for making stone tools. Jack Cresson is an expert in flintknapping, the art of making stone spear and arrow points, knives, and other tools. He has tested almost every species of tree found in the Pine Barrens, and finds that billets made from dogwood or persimmon are durable, effective, and hold up well under prolonged use. The spear points he makes with these billets are indistinguishable from the ancient tools made by the Lenape and their predecessors. (Cresson 1994, 1997; Regensburg, conversations over many years). Both archaeologists recognize hickory saplings as excellent material for spear and arrow shafts, and larger hickory as wood for axe, adze, and knife handles.

We know the Lenape made a variety of cordage, textiles, and baskets, from impressions the fibers made on pottery. They used our local vines, willow, and fibrous bark in addition to local grasses, sedges, and rushes. They made mats to be used as floor covering and as sheathing for their wigwams, and to line their storage pits. Smaller baskets were also employed as containers. String and twine were used to make fish nets and to decorate pottery. The Penobscots of Maine, another Algonkian tribe, still make exquisite baskets using geometrical designs and symbols typical of the decorations on Lenape ceramics found in local prehistoric sites.

The prehistoric Lenape of the Pine Barrens and New Jersey coast were not horticulturists but depended on a range of forest game, such as turkey, venison, and bear; fish, especially migratory species like herring and eels; and oysters, clams, and whelk. Many of these animal foods were smoked for later use or trade. There is much evidence of hickory nuts as a preferred staple food. Fruits were eaten fresh in season or dried, then mixed with dried meat and rendered fat to make the storage staple food "pemmican." All these foods were supplemented by herbaceous species used as tubers or as greens.

However, the Pine Barrens were also the Lenape drug store. Almost every woody species had medicinal uses; adding in the Pine Barrens' herbaceous plants would expand the list even further. Lenape from outside the Pine Barrens to the north, or the inner coastal plain to the west, traveled here to collect medicines. Finally, certain plants had ceremonial, rather than practical uses. Basswood, *Tilia,* was preferred by Algonkian tribes, including the Lenape, for the masks or "false faces" worn in religious ceremonies. Winged sumac is mentioned as a ceremonial beverage, and leaves or bark of several species were used for smoke or incense, in addition to tobacco.

The Pine Barrens were essentially uninhabited during much of the colonial period. Smallpox and other diseases decimated both the Lenape and early Swedish and Dutch settlers. While English colonists were not using the woody species for the range of purposes the Lenape had, the British exploited the Pine Barrens' timber species for export, local construction, and fuel. After the virgin timber was gone, by the early eighteenth century, the land was burned to promote grass and leased for cattle ranching—with poor success. When ranching was abandoned, pitch pine expanded its range as a major component of the second-growth forest.

Historic archaeologist Budd Wilson has studied the industries of the Pine Barrens (Wilson 1978). He reports that Batsto Furnace, manufacturing glass and bog iron products from Revolutionary War times to the Civil War, used twenty thousand acres of pitch pine timber to make charcoal as its industrial fuel. A thousand acres of pitch pine a year were cut and processed. After five or six cycles of clear-cutting and charcoaling, soils became so depleted that tree growth was stunted to the point that Batsto Furnace could no longer derive sufficient charcoal from its own acreage. At this point the original owners, the Richards family, sold the land to the Whartons, who used the mansion as a summer home. Eventually New Jersey acquired the "Wharton Tract" as part of its state forest system. Budd Wilson also has excavated other small charcoal kilns scattered over the Pine Barrens, as charcoaling was an important local industry through the nineteenth century and up until the 1950s.

Timber continued to be a major Pine Barrens export from the late eighteenth century to the present. Peter Wacker (1979) cites millions of board feet of timber shipped out of Somers Point, Atlantic County, from the Great Egg Harbor River system. Old-growth pitch pine was used for boards, while oak and chestnut were cut into beams and rafters. Many species supplied wood for shipyards from Toms River to Cape May; and even poor-quality cordwood was used as fuel for early steamboats. Shipbuilding was a major industry of the coastal towns. In Atlantic County, the Van Sant-Frambes shipyard built ocean-going merchant sailing ships from 1800 to 1889, when they could no longer compete with iron steamships. Later, the Van Sant shipyard, and other small ship builders, continued in business producing lifeguard dories, sneak boxes for waterfowl hunting, and small sailboats for clamming and fishing. The twentieth-century shipbuilders, such as Pacemaker, Egg Harbor Boat, and Viking Yachts, turned out luxury motorboats in which higher-quality timber was replaced by fiberglass and epoxy construction.

According to Atlantic County historian June Sheridan, agriculture thrived in nineteenth-century Pine Barrens towns such as Bargaintown, Hammonton, Warren Grove, Mays Landing, and Tabernacle, based on fertilizer imported from South America, transported in the locally built ships (pers. com., 1976). These included truck farms growing vegetables, and orchards growing peaches, apples, and grapes. Cranberries came into cultivation in the late nineteenth century, while our modern highbush blueberry cultivar was developed in the 1920s (Wacker 1979).

After World War II, the late Dr. Silas Little, working at the U.S. Northeast Forest Service Research Station in New Lisbon, New Jersey, made a valiant attempt to re-establish commercial forestry of genetically improved pitch pine and hybrid pitch-loblolly pines (Leydig and Little 1979). Dr. John Kuser of Rutgers University and Dr. George Zimmermann at Richard Stockton College are currently experimenting on improved strains and better forest management practice for Atlantic white cedar. Meanwhile, former boat builders in Egg Harbor City have established a new product. Tidewater Industries has become a leading manufacturer of garden furniture, settees, chairs, and tables made of our local white cedar. Their products are advertised in leading home and garden magazines.

However, with late-twentieth-century population growth threatening this area, combined with Pinelands Commission oversight, the Pine Barrens have a new role. The Pine Barrens have long interested hikers, with groups such as the Philadelphia Hiking Club using the Batona trail, birdwatchers, with activities sponsored by the New Jersey Audubon society, and canoeists paddling our rivers. Kayaking is the latest recreational activity gaining popularity in Pine Barrens waters. Thus, ecotourists are the latest people using and appreciating our Pine Barrens plants.

Sadly, while many groups, including the Pinelands Commission, the Pinelands Preservation Alliance, the Nature Conservancy, and the Sierra Club, are endeavoring to save and preserve the plant species of this unique biome, cultures of the Pine Barrens have fared less well. The Lenape language and culture are near extinction. The historic folk culture of late-nineteenth- and twentieth-century "Pineys" is essentially gone as old-timers pass away or leave New Jersey to seek homes in less crowded areas. The foremost Lenape ethnographer and scholar, Dr. Herbert Kraft of Seton Hall University, and a local Lenape leader and scholar, James Lonebear Revey, both died recently. We are fortunate that Gladys Tantaquidgeon (1972) and Dr. George Still, "the black doctor of the Pines," preserved some of the Lenape folk wisdom. Hopefully a new generation of ethnographers will be inspired to capture a more permanent record of our cultural heritage before the rich folk knowledge of our plants is lost forever.

Chapter 11

A Sense of Place

My hometown left me with a clear, and lingering, sense of place. In Albany, New York, in a neighborhood of row houses and small backyards, the country seemed to bask in blissful ignorance in the years following World War II. We were unaware of the dangers that could befall young boys as they skylarked through the parks and downtown shopping districts. My home range extended throughout the city and included Lincoln and Washington Parks as well as the State Museum on the fifth floor of the State Education Building. There, my curiosity about and love for living things was nourished by some kind and tolerant people.

For vacations, my family would travel to visit my uncle's family in rural upstate New York. Cobbleskill was a classic upstate town surrounded by small dairy farms, and the whole county could have been a template for Norman Rockwell. Returning to Albany, we'd all wait silently in the car until that exact moment when we crossed the city line. The smooth pavement would change abruptly as we crossed onto the cobblestone streets of Albany. At the time, the city was controlled by one of the last and most durable political machines in the country. Clearly, the politicos who ran Albany must have had more important things on their financial agenda than fixing the city streets. Because of that, the car would lurch as we dropped from the smooth pavement of the state highway and begin to rumble as we hit the cobblestones, occasionally jarring as we hit the potholes that marked the city streets. We'd all yell, "Al-bany!" and explode into giggles.

That time and that place are long gone. The city was remade during the administration of Governor Nelson Rockefeller, and many of the neighborhoods that I knew so well were replaced by plazas and administrative buildings. Likewise, many of the people who left their impressions on me are gone or lost. Yet, on those rare occasions when I return to Albany, someplace in the corner of my mind a little boy's voice sings, "Al-bany." I am completely comfortable walking those streets that are so strangely familiar yet so changed because I have a sense of place about Albany.

Today, I live in the Pine Barrens, an area very different from the Albany of my youth. Curiously, there are some similarities. Outside of Albany, there is a small pine barrens, called "The Pine Bush," where I used to spend time fishing with my father and my uncle. It was there where I hunted for rare plants with Dr. Stanley Smith, who was a botanist for the state of New York. Whether those experiences imprinted on me, or whether I have lived here so long that the New Jersey Pinelands has really become home, I cannot say. What I do know is that now when I return to the Pine Barrens, I feel like I am coming home.

Going home to the New Jersey Pine Barrens is like returning to Albany in another way. Both involve crossing a line. Although the line marking the entrance to the Pine Barrens is more diffuse than the sudden dip and rumble of the cobblestones of Albany, all of us cross a line as we travel into the Pine Barrens from outside because there is a shift in the vegetation and soils. The tall and more complex vegetation of the eastern deciduous forest transforms into the short, gnarly pines and oaks. The height of the shrub layer decreases, and white sand flashes through gaps in the ground cover like white skin through a green blouse. All these mark the beginning of the Pine Barrens. Today, travelling down the Garden State Parkway with my family, we repeat the ritual I had as a child as we sing out, "The Pin-ey Barrens!" as we cross that line.

I wonder whether my daughter, now a girl quickly moving into womanhood, will always hear herself silently sing out, "The Pin-ey Barrens" every time she crosses the line back to the place of her childhood. I wonder whether she will have a sense of place about these woods. Will the Pine Barrens remain largely unchanged, or will they become something akin to what the neighborhoods of Albany have become for me, places vaguely familiar but different. We shall see. The Pine Barrens are now protected, but those gains can always be lost. What is once lost is gone forever.

Transplanted as I have been from the woods of upstate New York, it took me a while to really see the Pine Barrens, to appreciate their beauty, to have their charm gradually take hold in me. These woods are very different from the forests with which I was familiar as a young man. Moreover, the Pine Barrens have much subtlety; they do not overwhelm. The Grand Canyon, the northern California coast, the Rocky Mountains, or the Alps all possess a visual impact on a scale that assaults the senses. You cannot just stand there the first time you see any of these wonders and not be moved even if you've seen their images in thousands of pictures and dozens of films. Maybe the complexity of color and form of these places humbles us. Maybe it is the vistas, the expanse of the view toward the horizon, the depth of the place compared to the sky. Maybe it is the sense of scale, the realization that you are a small part of a very big world.

What is clear is that the Pine Barrens are nothing like these places. For one thing, you can seldom see a visible horizon. The density and the height of the trees and shrubs conspire with the flat terrain to limit vision sometimes to within a few hundred feet. And then, the Pine Barrens are monotonous. There is little relief and few species. Standing in a pine woods where trees are mostly forty feet tall is hardly humbling compared to being in a redwood forest or even in a stand of mature white pines in New England. It takes time for the Pine Barrens to grab you, but grab you they do.

First, there is the water. Small, slow streams lace through the Pine Barrens. In their shallows, the water makes the sand seem red. As the water deepens, it quickly darkens, hiding the bottom from view. Unlike the clear dash of a mountain stream, the current of our dark-eyed streams is slow and inevitable. Even in summer, the water is cool because most of it emerges from the ground. In the smaller streams, fallen trees overhang the banks or crisscross the stream. Turtles are common; water snakes, herons, beaver, ospreys less so. The lucky traveler might see beaver, perhaps glance at a fox or even an otter. Summer weekends attract visitors from nearby cities, and canoe rental shops carry tourists down dirt roads to a stream and collect them again farther downriver. But during our long, warm autumns, you can travel by canoe or kayak down these streams and rarely see another visitor. On summer nights, you can glide over dark waters while bats sweep the air above you, filling the sky with sounds you cannot hear.

Then there are the forests that seem to enclose you, limiting your vision to a radius of maybe one hundred feet. In the uplands, the tangle of pine limbs and shrubs surrounds you. The trees are scattered, thin, and twisted, sometimes covered with lichens. The forest floor is largely obscured by a dense mat of shrubs. Light green lichens, grasses and ferns, pine needles, and sand cover the few open areas. In a cedar swamp, trees grow straight, thin, and tall, their bark spiraling upwards into the canopy high above. The cedars grow so close together that they block out the light, and the few scattered shrubs stretch upward above the carpet of moss and ferns, trying to reach beyond the dimness.

There is no horizon, no humbling sense of space. A walk in a dense pine woods or through a cedar swamp can be disorienting. It is easy to get lost in the Pine Barrens. But the enveloping woods do create a sense of solitude. You can travel down a stream or a trail and not see another person. Often, you cannot see a house, a power line, or a road even if they are only fifty feet away. Jack Cervetto of Warren Grove described the solitude perfectly over twenty years ago. "If you get right in the middle of a cedar swamp with a good growth of cedar, you really think that you're the only person in the world. You're closed in there in a way that gives you the feeling that there's nobody else around" (Berger and Sinton 1985, 121). It is almost like being transported back to an earlier time, and it is easy to imagine yourself in the forest primeval. Of course, that feeling is an illusion. The Pine Barrens are not untouched. But it is still very much a natural place.

It is easy to sit quietly in the pines and feel part of the natural world. All too often we feel apart from what is around us. We are surrounded by people and the everyday focus of our lives, and it is easy to have the sense that there is me, and then there is everything else outside of me. But here in the Pines, it is possible to feel a part of the place—a very small part of it all. And that feeling is not an illusion. It is real. That other sense, that we are apart from what is around us—that is the illusion.

My sense of place for Albany was imprinted upon me as a child. The place speaks to me in ways that I can feel but not really understand. My sense of place for the Pine Barrens grew in me much later in life. And I think I know why it draws me so.

Bibliography

Berger, J., and J. W. Sinton. 1985. *Water, Earth, and Fire: Land Use and Environmental Planning in the New Jersey Pine Barrens.* Baltimore: Johns Hopkins University Press.

Britton, N. L., and H. A. Brown. 1970. *An Illustrated Flora of the Northern United States and Canada.* 3 vols. New York: Dover Publications.

Burke, N. H. 2001. Personal communication.

Cavallo, J., and R. A. Mounier. 1981. "Aboriginal Settlement Patterns in the New Jersey Pinelands." In *History, Culture, and Archaeology of the Pine Barrens: Essays from the Third Pine Barrens Conference,* edited by J. W. Sinton and S. Hartzog. Pomona, N.J.: Stockton State College.

Collins, B. R. 1988. "The Backdrop for Pinelands Legislation." In *Protecting the New Jersey Pinelands: A New Direction in Land Use Management,* edited by B. R. Collins and E.W.B. Russell. New Brunswick: Rutgers University Press.

Collins, B. R., N. F. Good, and R. E. Good. 1988. "The Landscape of the New Jersey Pine Barrens." In *Protecting the New Jersey Pinelands: A New Direction in Land Use Management,* edited by B. R. Collins and E.W.B. Russell. New Brunswick: Rutgers University Press.

Collins, B. R., and E.W.B. Russell. 1988. "Protecting the New Jersey Pinelands." In *Protecting the New Jersey Pinelands: A New Direction in Land Use Management,* edited by B. R. Collins and E.W.B. Russell. New Brunswick: Rutgers University Press.

Conant, R. 1979. "A Zoological Review of the Amphibians and Reptiles of Southern New Jersey, with Emphasis on the Pine Barrens." In *Pine Barrens: Ecosystem and Landscape,* edited by R.T.T. Forman. New York: Academic Press.

Core, E. L., and N. P. Ammons. 1958. *Woody Plants in Winter.* Morgantown, W.V.: West Virginia University Press.

Cresson, J. 1994. "Platforms to Prehistory—Insights in Eastern Woodlands Lithotechnology." *Society for Primitive Technology Bulletin* 7:70–76.

———. 1997. "Eastern Hardwoods and Percussion Flaking." *Mammoth Trumpet* 12:20.

Douglas, L. A., and J. J. Trela. 1979. "Morphology of Pine Barrens Soils." In *Pine Barrens: Ecosystem and Landscape,* edited by R.T.T. Forman. New York: Academic Press.

Erichsen-Brown, C. 1979. *Medicinal and Other Uses of North American Plants.* New York: Dover Press.

Fairbrothers, D. E. 1979. "Endangered, Threatened, and Rare Vascular Plants of the Pine Barrens and Their Biogeography." In *Pine Barrens: Ecosystem and Landscape,* edited by R.T.T. Forman. New York: Academic Press.

Fernald, M. L. 1950. *Gray's Manual of Botany.* 8th ed. New York: American Book Co.

Ferren, W. R., Jr.; J. W. Braxton; and L. Hand. 1979. "Common Vascular Plants of the Pine Barrens." In *Pine Barrens: Ecosystem and Landscape,* edited by R.T.T. Forman. New York: Academic Press.

Foster, S., and J. A. Duke. 1990. *Peterson's Field Guide to Eastern and Central Medicinal Plants.* Boston: Houghton-Mifflin.

Gleason, H. A. 1962. *Plants in the Vicinity of New York.* New York: New York Botanical Garden, Hafner Publishing.

———, and A. Cronquist. 1963. *A Manual of Vascular Plants of Northeastern United States and Adjacent Canada.* New York: Van Nostrand-Reinhold.

Good, R. E., N. F. Good, and J. W. Anderson. 1979. "The Pine Barrens Plains." In *Pine Barrens: Ecosystem and Landscape,* edited by R.T.T. Forman. New York: Academic Press.

Harshberger, J. W. 1916. *The Vegetation of the New Jersey Pine Barrens: An Ecological Investigation.* Philadelphia: Christopher Sower.

Hartzog, S. H. 1981. "Palynology and Late Pleistocene-Holocene Environment on the New Jersey Outer Coastal Plain." In *History, Culture, and Archaeology of the Pine Barrens: Essays from the Third Pine Barrens Conference,* edited by J. W. Sinton and S. Hartzog. Pomona, N.J.: Stockton State College.

Havens, A. V. 1979. "Climate and Microclimate of the New Jersey Pine Barrens." In *Pine Barrens: Ecosystem and Landscape,* edited by R.T.T. Forman. New York: Academic Press.

Herrick, J., and D. Snow, eds. 1995. *Iroquois Medicinal Botany.* Syracuse, N.Y.: Syracuse University Press.

Heusser, C. J. 1979. "Vegetational History of the Pine Barrens." In *Pine Barrens: Ecosystem and Landscape,* edited by R.T.T. Forman. New York: Academic Press.

Hough, M. Y. 1983. *New Jersey Wild Plants.* Harmony, N.J.: Harmony Press.

Isphording, W. C., and W. Lodding. 1969. "Facies Changes in Sediments of Miocene Age in New Jersey." In *Geology of Selected Areas in New Jersey and Eastern Pennsylvania and Guidebook of Excursions,* edited by S. Subitzky. New Brunswick: Rutgers University Press.

Kraft, H. C. 1986. *The Lenape: Archaeology, History and Ethnography.* Collections of the New Jersey Historical Society, vol. 21. Newark, N.J.: New Jersey Historical Society.

Kuser, J., and G. L. Zimmermann.1996. "Restoring Atlantic White-Cedar Swamps: Techniques for Propagation and Establishment." *Tree Planters' Notes* (USDA) 46:78–96.

Leydig, F. T., and S. Little. 1979. "Pitch Pine (*Pinus rigida Mill.*): Ecology, Physiology and Genetics." In *Pine Barrens: Ecosystem and Landscape,* edited by R.T.T. Forman. New York: Academic Press.

Little, S. 1979. "Fire and Plant Succession in the New Jersey Pine Barrens." In *Pine Barrens: Ecosystem and Landscape,* edited by R.T.T. Forman. New York: Academic Press.

Markley, M. L. 1979. " Soil Series of the Pine Barrens." In *Pine Barrens: Ecosystem and Landscape,* edited by R.T.T. Forman. New York: Academic Press.

McCormick, J. 1979. "The Vegetation of the New Jersey Pine Barrens." In *Pine Barrens: Ecosystem and Landscape,* edited by R.T.T. Forman. New York: Academic Press.

Moerman, D. 1998. *Native American Ethnobotany.* Portland, Ore.: Timber Press.

Muenscher, W. C. 1990. *Keys to Woody Plants.* Ithaca, N.Y.: Comstock.

New Jersey Pinelands Commission. 1980. *Comprehensive Management Plan for the Pinelands National Reserve and Pinelands Area.* New Lisbon: The Pinelands Commission.

Owens, J. P., and N. F. Sohl. 1969. "Shelf and Deltaic Paleoenvironments in Cretaceous-Tertiary Formations of the New Jersey Coastal Plain." In *Geology of Selected Areas in New Jersey and Eastern Pennsylvania and Guidebook of Excursions,* edited by S. Subitzky. New Brunswick: Rutgers University.

Patrick, R., B. Matson, and L. Anderson. 1979. "Streams and Lakes in the Pine Barrens." In *Pine Barrens: Ecosystem and Landscape,* edited by R.T.T. Forman. New York: Academic Press.

Petrides, G. A. 1972. *A Field Guide to Trees and Shrubs.* Boston: Houghton Mifflin.

Regensburg, R. 1978. "Evidence of Indian Settlement Patterns in the Pine Barrens." In *Natural and Cultural Resources of the New Jersey Pine Barrens,* edited by J. W. Sinton. Stockton State College, Pomona, N.J.

Rhodehamel, E. C. 1979a. "Geology of the Pine Barrens of New Jersey." In *Pine Barrens: Ecosystem and Landscape,* edited by R.T.T. Forman. New York: Academic Press.

———. 1979b. "Hydrology of the New Jersey Pine Barrens." In *Pine Barrens: Ecosystem and Landscape,* edited by R.T.T. Forman. New York: Academic Press.

Richards, H. G. 1960. "The Geological History of the New Jersey Pine Barrens." *New Jersey Nature News* 15:146–151.

Russell, E.W.B. 1988. "Federal and State Pinelands Legislation." In *Protecting the New Jersey Pinelands: A New Direction in Land Use Management,* edited by B. R. Collins and E.W.B. Russell. New Brunswick: Rutgers University Press.

Sheridan, J. 1981. Personal communication.

Still, C. 1998. *Botany and Healing: Medicinal Plants of New Jersey.* New Brunswick: Rutgers University Press.

Stone, W. *The Plants of Southern New Jersey with Special Reference to the Flora of the Pine Barrens and the Geographic Distribution of Species.* Trenton, N.J.: Part II of the Annual Report of the New Jersey State Museum for 1910, 1911. Boston: Quarterman Publications, 1973.

Tantaquidgeon, G. 1972. *Folk Medicine of the Delaware and Related Algonkian Indians.* Harrisburg, Pa.: Pennsylvania Historic Commission.

Tedrow, J. C. 1979. "Development of Pine Barrens Soils." In *Pine Barrens: Ecosystem and Landscape,* edited by R.T.T. Forman. New York: Academic Press.

Wacker, P. O. 1979. "Human Exploitation of the New Jersey Pine Barrens before 1900." In *Pine Barrens: Ecosystem and Landscape,* edited by R.T.T. Forman. New York: Academic Press.

Whittaker, R. H. 1979. "Vegetational Relationships of the Pine Barrens." In *Pine Barrens: Ecosystem and Landscape,* edited by R.T.T. Forman. New York: Academic Press.

Wilson, B. 1978. "The Pine Barrens Glass Industry." In *Natural and Cultural Resources of the New Jersey Pine Barrens,* edited by J. W. Sinton. Pomona, N.J.: Stockton State College.

Windisch, A. G. 1999. "Fire Ecology of the New Jersey Pine Plains and Vicinity." Ph.D. dissertation, Rutgers: The State University of New Jersey.

Index of Terms

Note: Most of the following terms are explained in Chapter 2. In all three indices, italicized page numbers refer to illustrations.

Index of Common Names

Index of Scientific Names

About the Author

Michael D. Geller is an associate professor at Richard Stockton College of New Jersey. During his career, he has taught fourteen different courses in the Environmental Studies and Biology programs, and in General Studies. One of his hobbies is pen-and-ink drawing.